Date Due

301

TEN GREAT YEARS

STATISTICS OF THE ECONOMIC AND CULTURAL ACHIEVEMENTS OF
THE PEOPLE'S REPUBLIC OF CHINA

AMS PRESS

NEW YORK

TEN GREAT YEARS

STATISTICS OF THE ECONOMIC AND CULTURAL ACHIEVEMENTS OF THE PEOPLE'S REPUBLIC OF CHINA

Compiled by
THE STATE STATISTICAL BUREAU

FOREIGN LANGUAGES PRESS
PEKING 1960

Library of Congress Cataloging in Publication Data

China (People's Republic of China, 1949-   )
   Kuo chia t'ung chi chü.
   Ten great years.

   Translation of Wei ta ti shih nien.
   1. China (People's Republic of China, 1949-   )--
Statistics. I. Title.
[HA1701.A5513 1973]   315.1   72-38054
ISBN 0-404-56908-0

From the edition of 1960, Peking
First AMS edition published in 1973
Manufactured in the United States of America

AMS PRESS INC.
NEW YORK, N. Y.   10003

Foreword

Ten years have passed since the founding of the great People's Republic of China on October 1, 1949.

Ten years are but a moment in the course of man's historical development. But to the Chinese people, who in the past have gone through all kinds of tribulations and hardships, their experiences during these ten years have created an epic of world-shaking importance for ever worthy of being recalled. They are the Chinese people's ten years of rebirth; they are the Chinese people's ten years of progress at flying speed in economy and culture. During this short period the Chinese people, under the brilliant leadership of the Chinese Communist Party and Chairman Mao Tse-tung, with the help of the great Soviet Union and other fraternal socialist countries, and with the help and sympathy of the peace-loving peoples of the whole world, have worked with determination, diligence and great revolutionary drive. Over the wide expanse of their motherland, which was "poor and blank," they have written the newest and most beautiful words and printed the newest and most beautiful pictures where none existed before.

Ten years ago, just before the birth of the Chinese People's Republic, Chairman Mao Tse-tung made this prediction:

> The Chinese people will see that as soon as China's destiny is in their own hands, China, like the sun rising in the east, will radiate her own brilliant light over the earth, the mud and dirt left by the reactionary government will quickly be washed out, the wounds of war will be healed and a new, strong people's democratic republic of China will be founded both in name and in fact.

During the past ten years big strides were made in China's socialist revolution and socialist construction precisely as Chairman Mao predicted.

In the past decade socialist revolution and socialist construction in China passed through several different stages. The period from the founding of the People's Republic of China on October 1, 1949 to the end of 1952 was the period of the rehabilitation of the national economy. During those years the runaway inflation left by the reactionary Kuomintang government was stopped, market prices were stabilized and the task of rehabilitating the national economy which had been seriously damaged by the prolonged war was successfully fulfilled. This period also saw the completion, in the main, of the reform of the feudal system of landownership, the liberation of the productive forces in the countryside, the development of a socialist state economy, and the consolidation of the leadership of the state economy over the capitalist and individual economies. The period of the First Five-Year Plan for the development of the national economy extended from 1953 to 1957. During this period the socialist transformation of agriculture, handicrafts and capitalist industry and commerce was virtually completed and a great rectification campaign and a struggle against the bourgeois rightists were carried out. Thus a decisive victory was scored in the socialist revolution in the economic, political, as well as ideological spheres, and the social productive forces were further liberated. Besides, economic construction was carried out in a planned way and on a hitherto unknown scale which led to the successful fulfilment of the First Five-Year Plan for the development of the national economy and laid preliminary foundations for socialist industrialization.

In 1958 China entered a new era of development in socialist revolution and construction — an era of an all-round big leap forward in socialist construction with technical and cultural revolutions as the core. Under the inspiration of the general line — to go all out, aim high, and achieve greater. quicker, better and more economical results in building socialism — advanced by the Central Committee of the Chinese Communist Party and Chairman Mao Tse-tung, the Chinese people, with great determination and enthusiasm, made an all-round big leap forward in economic and cultural development such as had not been known in the history of China, and established people's communes in all rural areas. The characteristics of this period may be summarized in the words of Chairman Mao Tse-tung:

> Throughout the country, the communist spirit is surging forward. The political consciousness of the masses is rising rapidly. Backward sections among the masses have roused themselves energetically to catch up with the more advanced and this shows that China is forging ahead in her socialist economic revolution (where transformation of the relations of production has not yet been completed) as well as in her political, ideological, technical and cultural revolutions. In view of this, our country may not need as much time as was previously envisaged to catch up with the big capitalist countries in industrial and agricultural production.

During the past ten years the social and economic structure, the national economy, and the people's mental outlook have all undergone tremendous and profound changes. Private ownership of the means of production has practically been eliminated, class exploitation, which was practised for thousands of years, has been ended, and the socialist system has been firmly established. A new, independent and complete system of national economy is taking shape, the foundations of socialist industrialization have been laid, industrial and agricultural production is increasing by leaps and bounds and the productive capacity which was newly developed within the past ten years already surpasses that which had been developed during thousands of years. With the development of production the level of the people's material and cultural life has been raised considerably. The people's thoughts, understanding and outlook have taken on an entirely new character. They have great confidence and full belief in the happy life of socialism and communism.

These solid facts conclusively prove the great superiority of the socialist system. They prove that once the oppressed and enslaved working people break the fetters put on them by the reactionary ruling class and become the masters of their own destiny, they can evoke an immense, unfathomable store of energy. The wisdom and power of an emancipated people are inexhaustible. Under the inspiration and leadership of the Chinese Communist Party and Chairman Mao Tse-tung, under the inspiration and guidance of the general line, the people in their wisdom and strength are like a powerful army charging ahead and which no force can stop.

Imperialist elements, headed by the American imperialists, have always been extremely inimical to our revolution. They use all kinds of contemptible means to sabotage it. In recent years they have been shouting themselves hoarse to slander and maliciously attack our general line, our big leap forward, and our people's commune movement to attain their aim of sabotaging our cause, but their efforts have been in vain. In the past they have been powerless to stop the Chinese people from marching forward in giant strides in their work of revolution and construction, and in the future they will be still more powerless to prevent the Chinese people from marching forward triumphantly in accordance with their own will.

During the past ten years of economic and cultural development China has accomplished feats unheard of in her history. Her achievements are very great. But because China was very backward economically in the past, despite these achievements, her production today still remains at a comparatively low level, her industry is not sufficiently developed in size and extent, and her agricultural production does not yet fully meet the increasing needs of the people and of industry. Thus, the achievements to date still fall far below the great ideals of the

Chinese people. To completely change the condition of being "poor and blank" the Chinese people have to make yet greater efforts. At present the 650 million Chinese people, guided by the general line advanced by the Central Committee of the Chinese Communist Party and Chairman Mao, and encouraged by the 1958 big leap forward and the victory of the people's communes, are enthusiastically responding to the great call of the Eighth Plenary Session of the Eighth Central Committee of the Chinese Communist Party. Therefore they are struggling to make a continued leap forward in the national economy in 1959, so as to fulfil the main targets originally set down in the Second Five-Year Plan three years ahead of schedule in 1959. They are struggling to make China a great socialist country as quickly as possible with a highly developed modern industry, agriculture, science and culture.

The aim of this book is to describe, through extensive statistical data presented systematically, the great economic and cultural achievements of the People's Republic of China during the past decade.

Contents

CHARTS

Conversion Table

1 *mou* = 0.0667 hectare or 0.1647 acre

1 *tan* = 0.0500 ton or 0.0492 English ton

1 catty = 0.5000 kilogramme or 1.1023 pounds

AREA OF CHINA

9.6 million square kilometres

Population

(at year-end in millions)

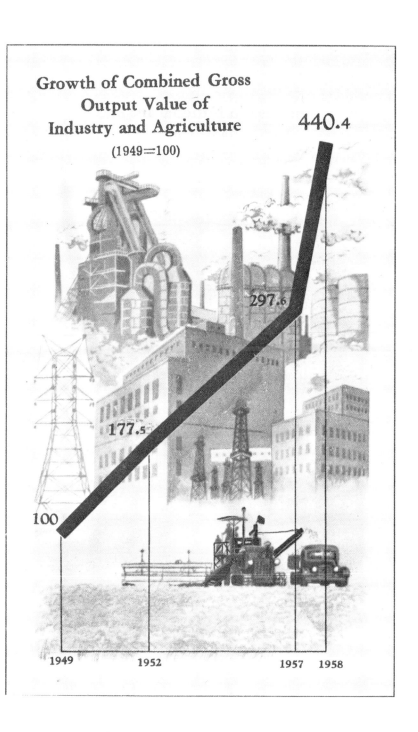

Growth of Combined Gross
Output Value of
Industry and Agriculture
(1949=100)

440.4

297.6

177.5

100

1949   1952   1957   1958

Increase in National Income

(1949=100)

348

260

170

100

1949   1952   1957 1958

Changes in Proportion of National Income by Economic Sector

(percentage)

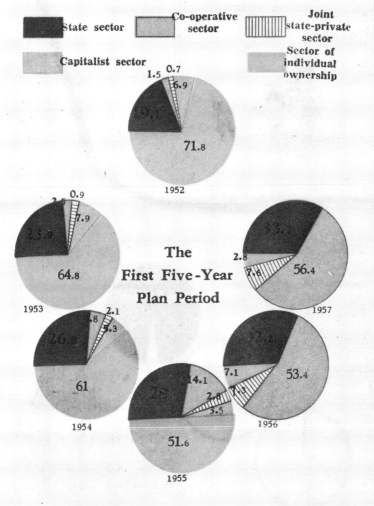

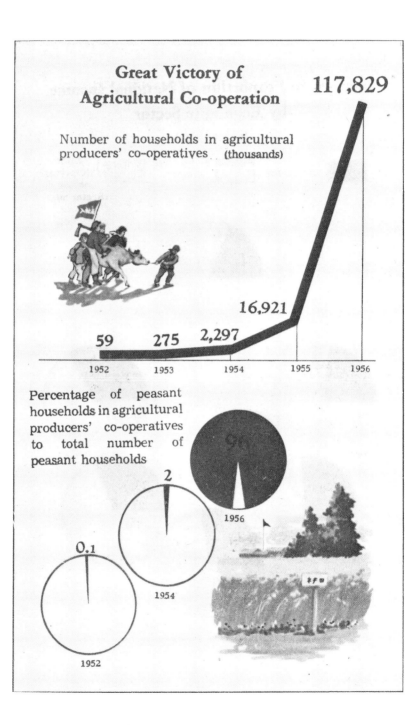

Great Victory of Agricultural Co-operation

Number of households in agricultural producers' co-operatives (thousands)

117,829

16,921

59 275 2,297

1952 1953 1954 1955 1956

Percentage of peasant households in agricultural producers' co-operatives to total number of peasant households

0.1
1952

2
1954

96
1956

Great Victory of Handicraft Co-operation

Increase in number of handicraft workers
taking part in co-operatives (thousands)

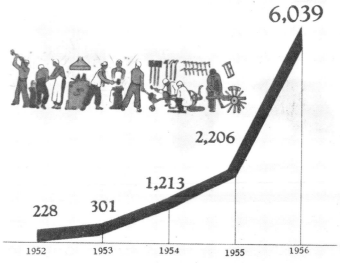

6,039

2,206

1,213

228   301

1952   1953   1954   1955   1956

Percentage of handicraft workers in co-operatives
to total number of handicraft workers

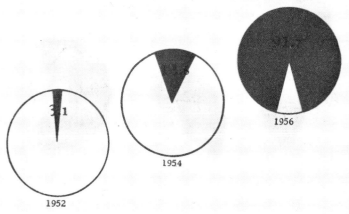

3.1

1952

1954

91.7

1956

Great Victory of Socialist Transformation of Capitalist Industry

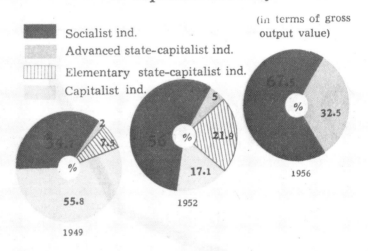

Socialist ind.

Advanced state-capitalist ind.

Elementary state-capitalist ind.

Capitalist ind.

(in terms of gross output value)

1949 — 34.7, 2, 7.5, 55.8 %

1952 — 56, 5, 21.9, 17.1 %

1956 — 67.5, 32.5 %

Great Victory of Socialist Transformation of Private Commerce

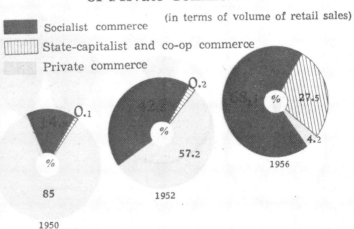

Socialist commerce

State-capitalist and co-op commerce

Private commerce

(in terms of volume of retail sales)

1950 — 14, 0.1, 85 %

1952 — 42, 0.2, 57.2 %

1956 — 68, 27.5, 4.2 %

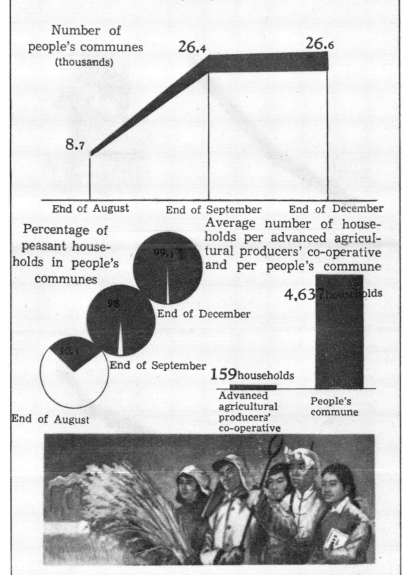

Great Victory of People's Commune Movement

(1958)

Number of people's communes (thousands)

26.4   26.6

8.7

Ehd of August   End of September   End of December

Percentage of peasant house-holds in people's communes

Average number of house-holds per advanced agricultural producers' co-operative and per people's commune

99.1

End of December

98

End of September

30.4

End of August

4,637 households

159 households

Advanced agricultural producers' co-operative

People's commune

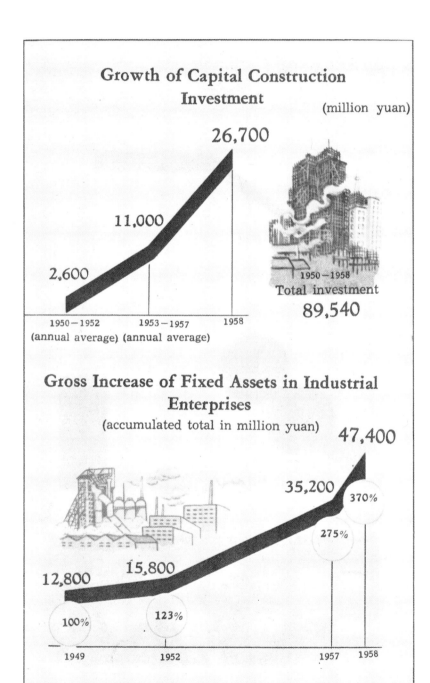

Growth of Capital Construction Investment

(million yuan)

26,700

11,000

2,600

1950—1952 (annual average)   1953—1957 (annual average)   1958

1950—1958
Total investment
89,540

Gross Increase of Fixed Assets in Industrial Enterprises

(accumulated total in million yuan)

47,400

35,200

370%

275%

12,800   15,800

100%   123%

1949   1952   1957   1958

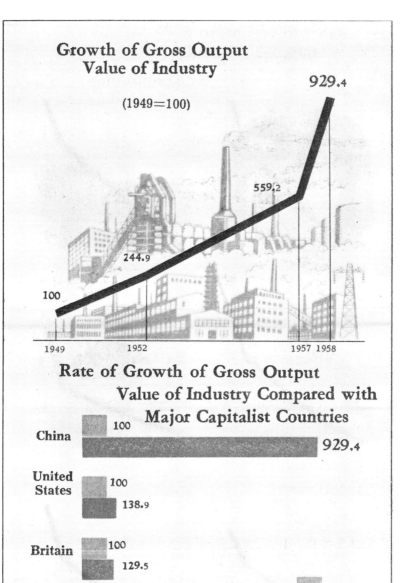

Growth of Gross Output Value of Industry

(1949=100)

929.4

559.2

244.9

100

1949　　1952　　　　　　1957 1958

Rate of Growth of Gross Output Value of Industry Compared with Major Capitalist Countries

China
100
929.4

United States
100
138.9

Britain
100
129.5

France
100
186.6

1949
1958

(1949=100)

Growth of Output of Major
Industrial Products (I) (1949=100)

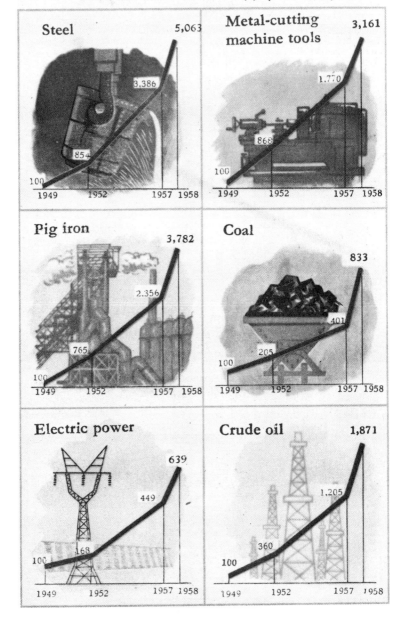

Steel
5,063
3,386
854
100
1949 1952 1957 1958

Metal-cutting machine tools
3,161
1,770
868
100
1949 1952 1957 1958

Pig iron
3,782
2,356
765
100
1949 1952 1957 1958

Coal
833
401
205
100
1949 1952 1957 1958

Electric power
639
449
168
100
1949 1952 1957 1958

Crude oil
1,871
1,205
360
100
1949 1952 1957 1958

Growth of Output of Major Industrial Products (II)

(1949=100)

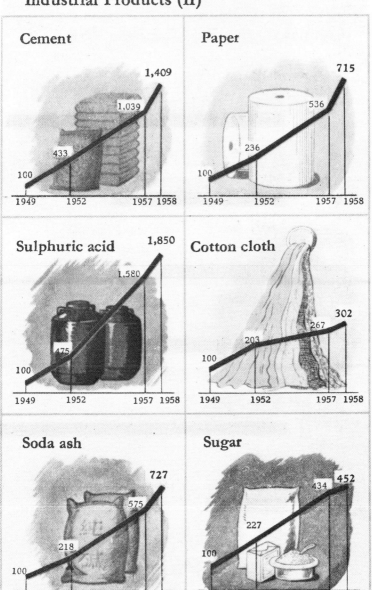

Cement

1,409
1,039
433
100

1949　1952　　1957 1958

Paper

715
536
236
100

1949　1952　　1957 1958

Sulphuric acid

1,850
1,580
475
100

1949　1952　　1957 1958

Cotton cloth

302
267
203
100

1949　1952　　1957 1958

Soda ash

727
575
218
100

1949　1952　　1957 1958

Sugar

452
434
227
100

1949　1952　　1957 1958

Output of Major Industrial Products Compared with Pre-Liberation Peak Year

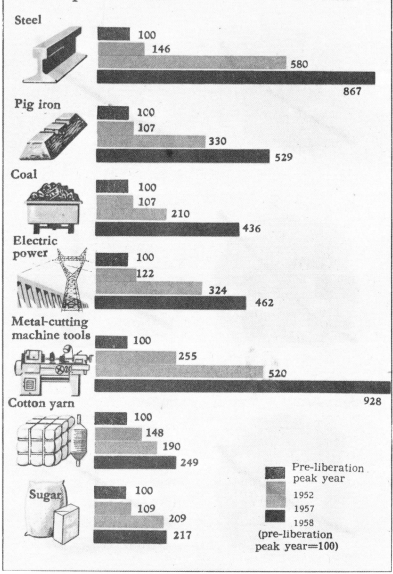

Steel
100
146
580
867

Pig iron
100
107
330
529

Coal
100
107
210
436

Electric power
100
122
324
462

Metal-cutting machine tools
100
255
520
928

Cotton yarn
100
148
190
249

Sugar
100
109
209
217

Pre-liberation peak year
1952
1957
1958
(pre-liberation peak year=100)

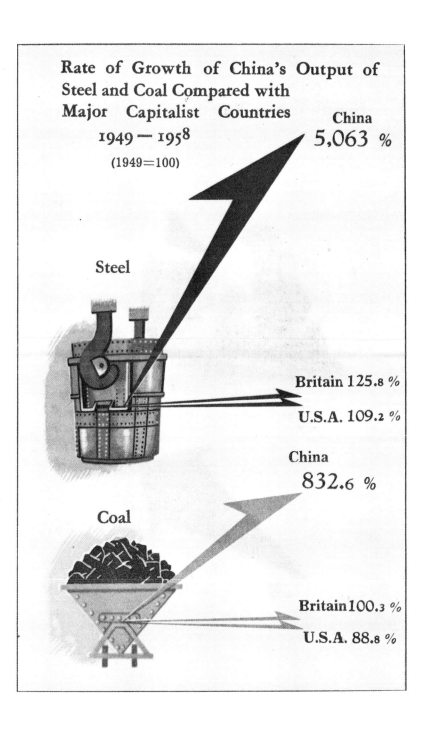

Rate of Growth of China's Output of Steel and Coal Compared with Major Capitalist Countries 1949 — 1958

(1949=100)

China
5,063 %

Steel

Britain 125.8 %

U.S.A. 109.2 %

China
832.6 %

Coal

Britain 100.3 %

U.S.A. 88.8 %

Rise in Labour Productivity in Industry

(workers and other employees in industrial enterprises at county level and above)

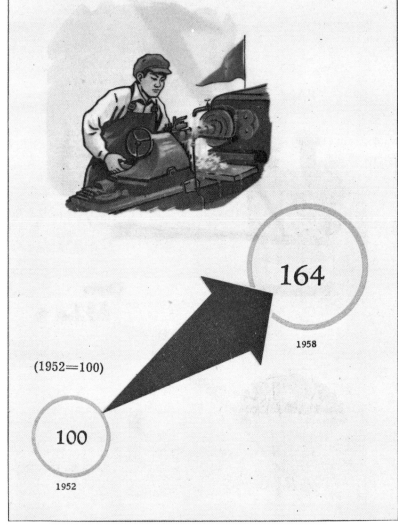

164

1958

(1952=100)

100

1952

Growth of Gross Output Value
of Agriculture
(1949=100)

100

148.5

185.1

231.4

1949   1952   1957   1958

Growth of Output of Grain and Cotton

(1949=100)

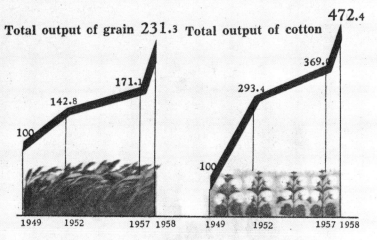

Total output of grain 231.3   Total output of cotton

472.4

171.1
142.8
100
369.0
293.4
100

1949 1952   1957 1958   1949   1952   1957 1958

Rate of Growth of Output of Grain and Cotton Compared with Major Capitalist Countries

(1949=100)

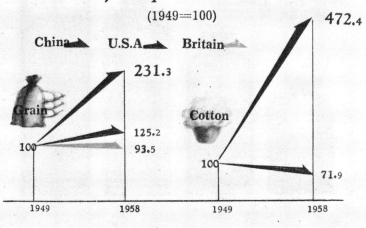

China ➤   U.S.A ➤   Britain

231.3

472.4

Grain
125.2
93.5
100

Cotton
100
71.9

1949   1958   1949   1958

Output of Grain and Cotton in 1958
Compared with Pre-Liberation Peak Year

Grain

500,000
(million catties)

1958

277,400
(million
catties)

Pre-liberation
peak year

Cotton

42
(million *tan*)

1958

16.98
(million
tan)

Pre-liberation
peak year

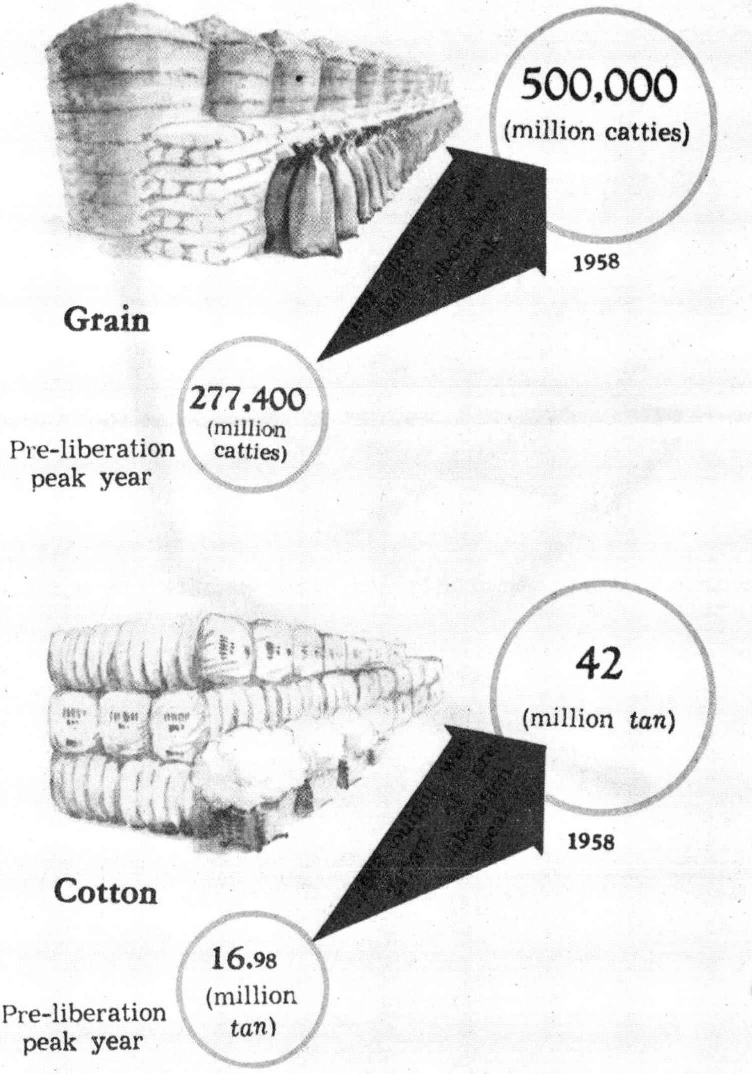

Increase in Area Under Irrigation

(accumulated area in million *mou*)

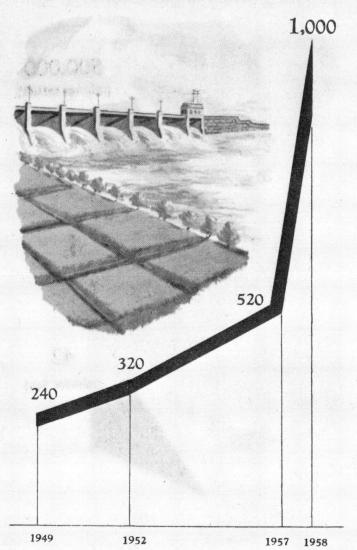

1,000

520

320

240

1949   1952   1957   1958

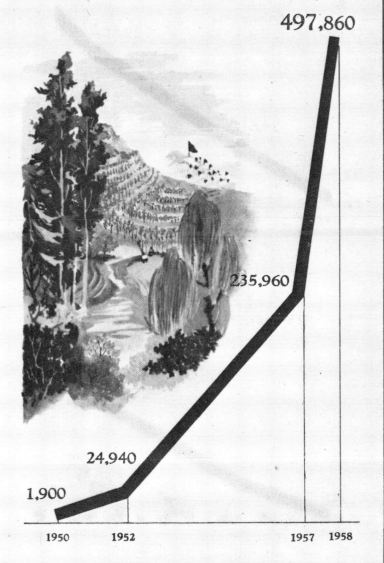

Expansion of Afforested Area

(accumulated area in thousand *mou*)

497,860

235,960

24,940

1,900

1950   1952   1957   1958

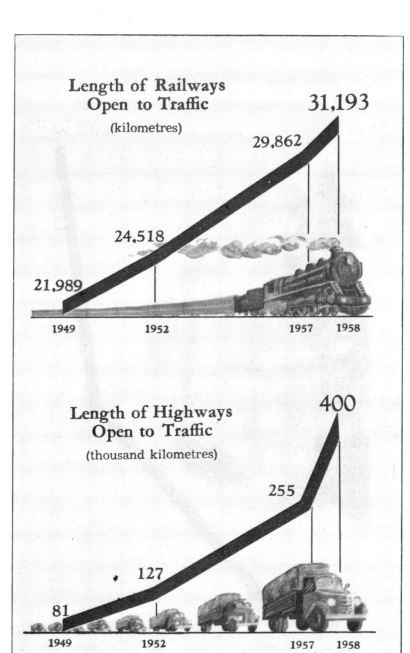

Length of Railways
Open to Traffic
(kilometres)

31,193

29,862

24,518

21,989

1949   1952   1957   1958

Length of Highways
Open to Traffic
(thousand kilometres)

400

255

127

81

1949   1952   1957   1958

Increase in Freight Ton-Kilometres Performed by Modern Means of Transport

(million ton-kilometres)

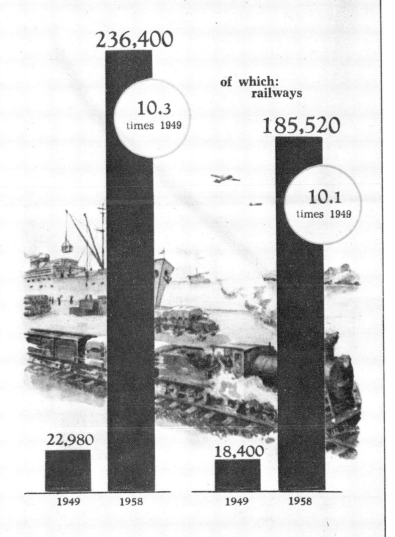

236,400

10.3
times 1949

of which:
railways

185,520

10.1
times 1949

22,980

1949   1958

18,400

1949   1958

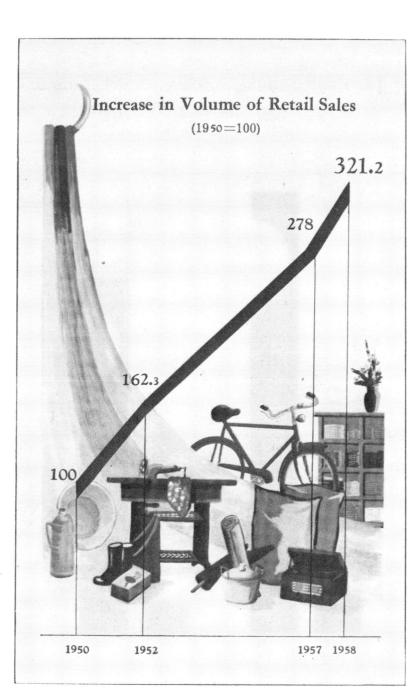

Increase in Volume of Retail Sales
(1950=100)

321.2

278

162.3

100

1950   1952   1957   1958

Increase in Number of Enrolled Students

(thousands)

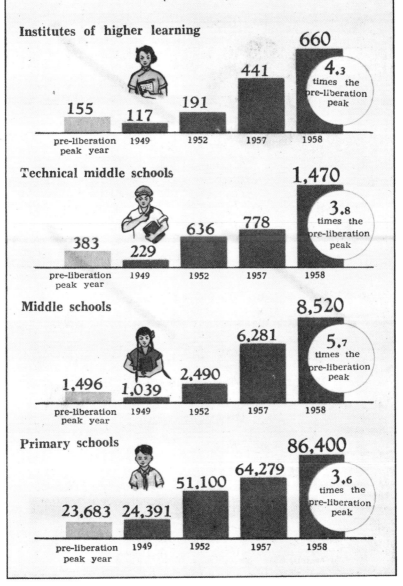

Institutes of higher learning

pre-liberation peak year	1949	1952	1957	1958
155	117	191	441	660

4.3 times the pre-liberation peak

Technical middle schools

pre-liberation peak year	1949	1952	1957	1958
383	229	636	778	1,470

3.8 times the pre-liberation peak

Middle schools

pre-liberation peak year	1949	1952	1957	1958
1,496	1,039	2,490	6,281	8,520

5.7 times the pre-liberation peak

Primary schools

pre-liberation peak year	1949	1952	1957	1958
23,683	24,391	51,100	64,279	86,400

3.6 times the pre-liberation peak

Increase in Number of Graduates
(thousands)

Institutes of higher learning

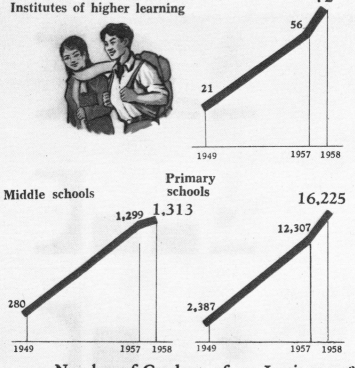

21	1949
56	1957
72	1958

Middle schools

Primary schools

280 · 1949
1,299 · 1957
1,313 · 1958

2,387 · 1949
12,307 · 1957
16,225 · 1958

Number of Graduates from Institutes of Higher Learning Compared with Pre-Liberation

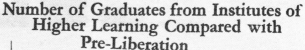

20 years before liberation
Annual av.
9,272
Of whom: engineering students
1,584

10 years after liberation
Annual av.
43,112
Of whom: engineering students
12,957

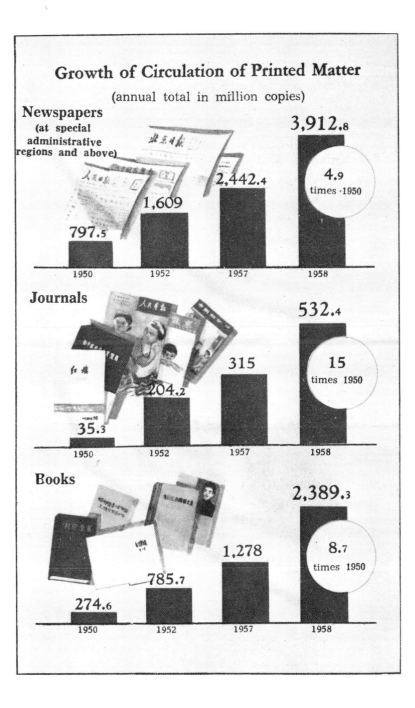

Growth of Circulation of Printed Matter

(annual total in million copies)

Newspapers
(at special
administrative
regions and above)

797.5 — 1950
1,609 — 1952
2,442.4 — 1957
3,912.8 — 1958

4.9 times 1950

Journals

35.3 — 1950
204.2 — 1952
315 — 1957
532.4 — 1958

15 times 1950

Books

274.6 — 1950
785.7 — 1952
1,278 — 1957
2,389.3 — 1958

8.7 times 1950

Growth of Cinema Industry

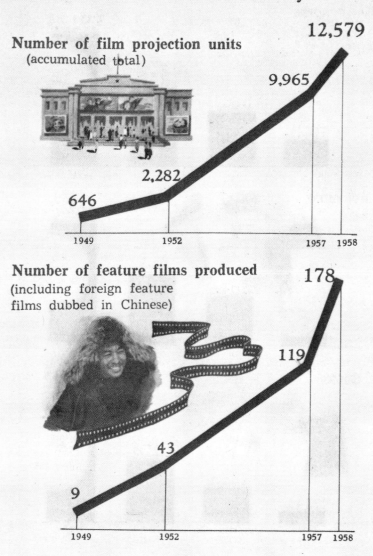

Number of film projection units
(accumulated total)

12,579

9,965

2,282

646

1949   1952   1957   1958

Number of feature films produced
(including foreign feature
films dubbed in Chinese)

178

119

43

9

1949   1952   1957   1958

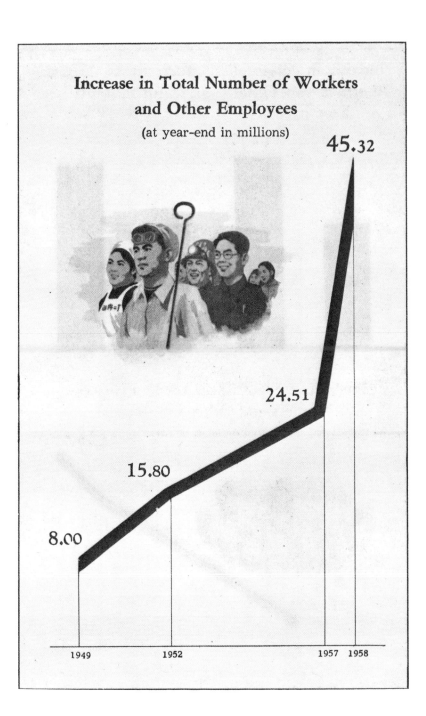

Increase in Total Number of Workers
and Other Employees
(at year-end in millions)

45.32

24.51

15.80

8.00

1949 1952 1957 1958

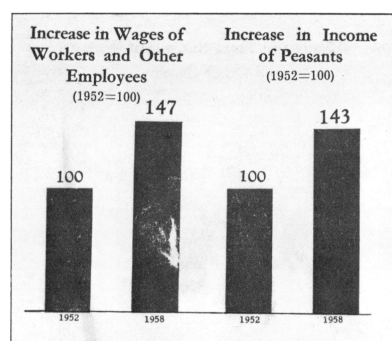

Increase in Wages of Workers and Other Employees

(1952=100)

100
1952

147
1958

Increase in Income of Peasants

(1952=100)

100
1952

143
1958

Increase in Floor Space for Housing for Workers and Other Employees

(accumulated total in thousand sq. m.)

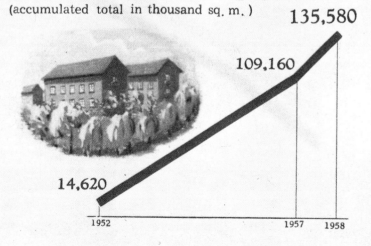

135,580

109,160

14,620

1952

1957

1958

Development of Public Health Services

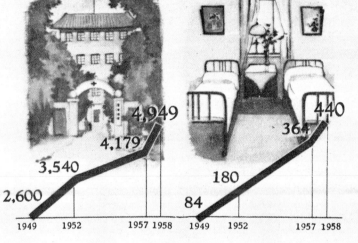

Number of hospitals

2,600 — 1949
3,540 — 1952
4,179 — 1957
4,949 — 1958

Number of beds in hospitals and sanatoria
(thousands)

84 — 1949
180 — 1952
364 — 1957
440 — 1958

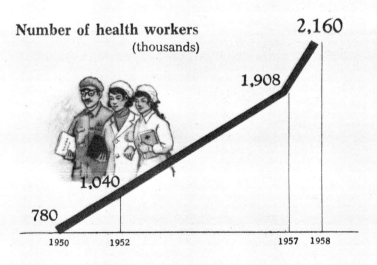

Number of health workers
(thousands)

780 — 1950
1,040 — 1952
1,908 — 1957
2,160 — 1958

I. THE GROWTH AND DEVELOPMENT OF THE PEOPLE'S REPUBLIC OF CHINA

China is known for her vast territory, rich natural resources, large population and long history. There are 22 provinces, including Taiwan which is to be liberated, 5 autonomous regions including the Tibetan Autonomous Region now in preparation, and 2 municipalities. She has a population of more than 650 million, or about one-fourth of mankind and an area of 9.6 million square kilometres, one-fourteenth of the world's total or the size of Europe. On this huge expanse of land there are over 1,600 million *mou* of arable land; 1,600 rivers covering the country like a spider's web and many lakes affording the people facilities for navigation and irrigation; a long coastline leading to many foreign countries; a rich variety of mineral resources, and so on.

History bears witness to the fact that China is one of the advanced countries of the world with the longest continuous economic and cultural history. Her history provable by written sources alone covers more than 4,000 years. But during the past one hundred years, owing to foreign imperialist aggression and the reactionary rule of the feudal landlord class and the bureaucrat-capitalist class, China gradually degenerated into a semi-colonial, semi-feudal country with a backward economy and culture and the people lived under exceedingly wretched conditions.

The economy of old China was very backward. Her industry remained at a very low stage of development and she had no heavy industry of her own. Agricultural production was as backward as in mediaeval times. Before liberation the highest annual production of steel in China was only 923,000 tons; of coal, 61,880,000 tons; of electric power, less than 6,000 million kwh; of grain, 277,400 million catties; and of cotton, less than 17 million *tan*. The backward economy of old China was not free from the scourge of destructive forces. During the wars launched against the Chinese people by the Japanese imperialists and Kuomintang reactionaries, which lasted for more than ten years, the country was seriously damaged. At the time of liberation in 1949, grain and soya bean production declined by 25 per cent and cotton production dropped by 48 per cent in comparison with the previous peak figures. Industrial production declined even more. Output of the means of production declined by 53 per cent and consumer goods decreased by 50 per cent. Compared with pre-liberation peak figures the percentage of the decreases in production of the following important items were: steel, 83 per cent; pig iron, 86 per cent; coal, 48 per cent; electric power, 28 per cent; cement, 71 per cent; cotton cloth, 32 per cent; and sugar, 52 per cent. These decreases, combined with the runaway inflation caused by the reactionary Kuomintang, reduced the living standards of the working people to a very low level.

Under the brilliant leadership of the Chinese Communist Party and Chairman Mao Tse-tung and after long and difficult revolutionary struggles, the courageous and industrious Chinese people eventually won the great victory of the people's democratic revolution in 1949, overthrew the reactionary rule of imperialism, feudalism, and bureaucrat-capitalism, and founded the great People's Republic of China which is led by the working class and is based on a worker-peasant alliance. From then on the Chinese people, numbering a quarter of the world's population, have stood up; semi-colonial, semi-feudal old China has gone for good; and the history of the development of the Chinese people has turned a new leaf. During the past ten years, under the guidance of the Chinese Communist Party and Chairman Mao Tse-tung, the Chinese people have displayed intense enthusiasm for work and great creative ability. They have recorded remarkable achievements in socialist construction while they were winning a speedy victory in socialist revolution. The backward state of the national economy inherited from old China has begun to show conspicuous changes.

As soon as the People's Republic of China was founded, measures were taken to abrogate the special privileges of the imperialists, and all enterprises of the bureaucrat-capitalists were confiscated and changed into enterprises of the socialist state economy which are owned by all the people. Meanwhile measures were also taken to heal the wounds of war and begin the difficult task of national economic rehabilitation. The latter task was successfully completed in three years. During the period 1949-1952 the gross output value of industry increased by 145 per cent and the gross output value of agriculture increased by 48.5 per cent. By 1952 most of the major products of industry and agriculture had either been restored to their previous levels or had actually surpassed pre-liberation records.

In 1953 the Central Committee of the Chinese Communist Party and Chairman Mao Tse-tung put forward the general line for the transition period: to gradually carry out the socialist industrialization and to gradually complete the socialist transformation of agriculture, handicrafts and capitalist industry and commerce over a fairly long period of time. Under the guidance of this general line the First Five-Year Plan for the development of the national economy was launched and its targets were successfully overfulfilled in 1957. During the period 1952-1957 the gross output value of industry increased by 128 per cent, an average annual increase of 18 per cent, and the gross output value of agriculture increased by 25 per cent, an annual increase of 4.5 per cent. Great progress was also made in other spheres of the economy as well as in culture. During the First Five-Year Plan the preliminary foundations were laid for socialist industrialization, and the socialist transformation of agriculture, handicrafts and capitalist industry and commerce was virtually completed.

[3]

The year 1958 was the first year of the Second Five-Year Plan for the development of the national economy, which was drafted on a much larger scale than the First Five-Year Plan. Under the guidance of the Party's general line of socialist construction and on the basis of the successful fulfilment of the First Five-Year Plan, the people of the whole country made an all-round big leap forward in the national economy to an extent unknown in the history of China. The combined gross output value of industry and agriculture increased by 48 per cent in one year, of which the increase in the gross output value of industry was 66 per cent, exceeding the total increase, in absolute terms, of the entire First Five-Year Plan period; the increase in gross output value of agriculture was 25 per cent, which was comparable to the total growth achieved in the First Five-Year Plan period. The increase in the main industrial and agricultural items was considerably greater than in any previous year. In 1958 investment in capital construction increased by a record 93 per cent. The all-round big leap forward in the national economy in 1958 not only greatly increased the material and technical base of China but also shortened the time required to build socialism.

In 1959 China's national economy continued to leap forward on the basis of the big leap forward of 1958. According to the readjusted plan proposed by the Eighth Plenary Session of the Eighth Central Committee of the Chinese Communist Party and adopted by the Standing Committee of the National People's Congress the gross output value of industry in 1959 will amount to 147,000 million yuan, an increase of 25.6 per cent over 1958. Steel production (not including production by indigenous methods) will amount to 12 million tons, an increase of 4 million tons or 50 per cent over 1958. Coal production will amount to 335 million tons, an increase of 65 million tons or 24 per cent over 1958. Although agricultural production has been seriously hampered by floods and drought, efforts will still be made to have grain and cotton production increase by about 10 per cent over 1958, a year

[4]

of unusually good harvests. During the big leap forward of 1958 the targets for 1962, as set down in the Second Five-Year Plan, for grain, coal, lumber and salt were already fulfilled. The successful carrying out of the plan for 1959 will enable the targets originally set for 1962 to be exceeded, reached or approximated by 1959 for the following items: steel, metallurgical equipment, power-generating equipment, metal-cutting machine tools, cotton yarn, machine-made paper and cotton. In other words, the main targets of the Second Five-Year Plan will be practically fulfilled three years ahead of schedule. The achievements made during the big leap forward of 1958 and the continued leap forward in 1959 make it possible to realize, in the main, the original goal to overtake Britain in 15 years in the quantity of the major items of industrial production in about ten years, and to overfulfil the targets of the 12-year Programme of Agricultural Development originally planned for fulfilment by 1967 considerably ahead of schedule.

The achievements made in socialist construction in the past decade are very great.

The productive capacity developed in the last ten years surpassed the total productive capacity that had been developed in China for several thousand years before liberation. From 1950 to 1958 the total investment in capital construction made by the government was 89,500 million yuan, a sum equivalent to the value of over 900 million *liang*[1] of gold. The value of new fixed assets amounted to 71,900 million yuan, of which industrial fixed assets added up to 34,360 million yuan, 2.7 times as much as the value of industrial fixed assets accumulated in the last one hundred years of old China. In 1958 the national income increased 250 per cent over the figures of 1949, an annual average increase of 14.9 per cent. In the same year the combined gross output value of industry and agriculture was 184,100 million yuan, an increase of 340

---

[1] 1 *liang*=31.2500 grammes.

per cent over 1949. Output of industry alone had a total value of 117,000 million yuan, an increase of 830 per cent over 1949 and the figure for agricultural production was 67,100 million yuan, an increase of 130 per cent over 1949. The increase in the main items of industrial and agricultural production was particularly large. Comparing production figures of 1958 with 1949, the following increases were recorded: steel (not including steel produced by indigenous methods) increased 4,960 per cent; pig iron (not including iron produced by indigenous methods) increased 3,680 per cent; electric power, 540 per cent; coal, 730 per cent; crude oil, 1,770 per cent; metal-cutting machine tools, 3,060 per cent; cement, 1,310 per cent; cotton cloth, 200 per cent; paper, 610 per cent; edible vegetable oil, 180 per cent; sugar, 350 per cent; grain, 130 per cent; and cotton, 370 per cent.

The pace of the development of China's national economy is something which no capitalist country could hope for. During the nine years, 1950-1958, the average annual increase in the gross output value of industry and in the gross output value of agriculture was 28.1 per cent and 9.8 per cent respectively. The average annual increases in the quantity of the major items of industrial and agricultural production were as follows: steel, 54.7 per cent; coal, 26.6 per cent; grain, 9.8 per cent; and cotton, 18.8 per cent. During the same period the average annual increase of industrial production in the U.S.A. was only 3.7 per cent, while steel increased only 1 per cent and grain only 2.5 per cent. There was no increase in coal and cotton, in fact, their output even declined. In the same period in Britain the average annual increase of industrial production was 2.9 per cent, steel, 2.6 per cent and coal, only 0.03 per cent, while grain output declined.

All this proves that the two different systems, socialism and capitalism, create two entirely different rates of development of the national economy and socialism is incomparably the better system.

The great achievements China has made during the past ten years in socialist revolution and construction have consolidated the people's democratic system, increased the solidarity between the peoples of various nationalities, and strengthened the socialist camp headed by the Soviet Union.

AREA AND POPULATION

Area (thousand sq. km.)	Population in 1957 (thousands)	Density of population (no. of persons per sq. km.)
9,597	656,630	68

POPULATION[1]

(thousands)

Year	Total population	Male	Female
1949	548,770	285,140	263,630
1953	595,550	308,850	286,700
1957	656,630	340,140	316,490

[1] At the year-end.   Chinese living in Hongkong, Macao and abroad are not included.

THE NATIONALITIES OF CHINA

Nationality	Main geographic distribution
Han	All provinces, municipalities and regions of China
Mongolian	Inner Mongolian Autonomous Region, Liaoning and other provinces
Hui	Ningsia Hui Autonomous Region, Kansu and other provinces
Tibetan	Tibet, Szechuan, Chinghai and other provinces
Uighur	Sinkiang Uighur Autonomous Region
Miao	Kweichow, Yunnan, Hunan and other provinces
Yi	Szechuan, Yunnan and other provinces
Chuang	Kwangsi Chuang Autonomous Region, Yunnan and other provinces
Puyi	Kweichow
Korean	Kirin and other provinces
Manchu	Liaoning, Kirin, Heilungkiang and other provinces
Tung	Kweichow and other provinces
Yao	Kwangsi Chuang Autonomous Region
Pai	Yunnan
Tuchia	Hunan and Hupeh
Kazakh	Sinkiang Uighur Autonomous Region
Hani	Yunnan
Tai	Yunnan
Li	Kwangtung
Lisu	Yunnan
Kawa	Yunnan
Yu	Fukien and Chekiang
Kaoshan	Taiwan
Tunghsiang	Kansu
Nasi	Yunnan
Lahu	Yunnan

Nationality	Main geographic distribution
Shui	Kweichow
Chingpo	Yunnan
Khalkha	Sinkiang Uighur Autonomous Region
Tu	Chinghai
Tahur	Inner Mongolian Autonomous Region and Heilungkiang
Molao	Kwangsi Chuang Autonomous Region
Chiang	Szechuan
Pulang	Yunnan
Sala	Chinghai
Russian	Sinkiang Uighur Autonomous Region
Chilao	Kweichow
Sibo	Sinkiang Uighur Autonomous Region
Maonan	Kwangsi Chuang Autonomous Region
Achang	Yunnan
Tadjik	Sinkiang Uighur Autonomous Region
Uzbek	Sinkiang Uighur Autonomous Region
Nu	Yunnan
Tartar	Sinkiang Uighur Autonomous Region
Owenke	Inner Mongolian Autonomous Region
Paoan	Kansu
Ching	Kwangtung
Yuku	Kansu
Penglung	Yunnan
Tulung	Yunnan
Olunchun	Inner Mongolian Autonomous Region and Heilungkiang
Hoche	Heilungkiang

POPULATION BY PROVINCES, AUTONOMOUS REGIONS AND MUNICIPALITIES

(year-end of 1957 in thousands)

Place	Population	Place	Population
Total	**656,630**		
Peking	4,010	Anhwei	33,560
Shanghai	6,900	Chekiang	25,280
Hopei	44,720	Fukien	14,650
Shansi	15,960	Honan	48,670
Inner Mongolian Aut. Region	9,200	Hupeh	30,790
Liaoning	24,090	Hunan	36,220
Kirin	12,550	Kiangsi	18,610
Heilungkiang	14,860	Kwangtung	37,960
Shensi	18,130	Kwangsi Chuang Aut. Region	19,390
Kansu	12,800	Szechuan	72,160
Ningsia Hui Aut. Region	1,810	Kweichow	16,890
Chinghai	2,050	Yunnan	19,100
Sinkiang Uighur Aut. Region	5,640	Tibet	1,270
Shantung	54,030	Taiwan	10,100
Kiangsu	45,230		

Note: Figures for Hopei, Kansu and Ningsia Hui Autonomous Region were taken according to the administrative divisions as they existed at the end of 1958. All the others were taken according to the administrative divisions as they existed at the end of 1957.

[11]

POPULATION OF CITIES HAVING OVER 500,000 INHABITANTS

(year-end of 1957 in thousands)

City	Population	City	Population
Municipalities directly under central authority:		Kiangsu	
		Nanking	1,419
		Hsuchow	676
Peking	4,010	Soochow	633
Shanghai	6,900	Wusih	613
Hopei		Chekiang	
Tientsin	3,220	Hangchow	784
Tangshan	800		
Shihchiachuang	598	Fukien	
		Foochow	616
Shansi			
Taiyuan	1,020	Honan	
		Chengchow	766
Liaoning			
Shenyang	2,411	Hupeh	
Lushun-Talien	1,508	Wuhan	2,146
Fushun	985		
Anshan	805	Hunan	
		Changsha	703
Kirin			
Changchun	975	Kiangsi	
Kirin	568	Nanchang	508
Heilungkiang		Kwangtung	
Harbin	1,552	Canton	1,840
Tsitsihar	668		
		Szechuan	
Shensi		Chungking	2,121
Sian	1,310	Chengtu	1,107
Kansu		Kweichow	
Lanchow	699	Kweiyang	504
Shantung		Yunnan	
Tsinan	862	Kunming	880
Tsingtao	1,121		
Tzupo	806		

GROWTH IN NUMBER OF BIG AND MEDIUM-SIZED CITIES

Population	No. of cities	
	1952	1957
Total	**159**	**176**
Over 5 million	1	1
3 to 5 million	—	2
1 to 3 million	8	11
0.5 to 1 million	15	20
100,000 to 500,000	81	90
Under 100,000	54	52

ADMINISTRATIVE DIVISIONS OF 1958
(from county upwards)

Administrative divisions	Number	Administrative divisions	Number
Municipalities directly under central authority	2	Municipalities	183
Provinces	22	County-level divisions:	1,747
Autonomous regions[1]	5	Counties	1,626
Autonomous *chou*	29	Autonomous counties Autonomous banners	} 54
Leagues[2]	7	Banners	48
Administrative regions	3		
Special administrative regions	121		

[1]The autonomous regions include the Tibetan Autonomous Region now in preparation.

[2]An administrative division corresponding to a special administrative region.

[13]

NUMBER OF DEPUTIES TO THE NATIONAL PEOPLE'S CONGRESS
(1959)

Total	**1,226**
Number of women deputies	150
Percentage of women deputies	12.2
Number of deputies from national minorities	179
Percentage of deputies from national minorities	14.6

NATURAL RESOURCES
(verified figures as of end of 1958)

1. Proved reserves[1]
   Iron ores   over 8,000 million tons
   Coal   over 80,000 million tons
2. Forests   about 100 million hectares
3. Potential hydro-electric capacity   580 million kw.

[1]These reserves can be used as a basis for designing capital construction and investment.

RAPID INCREASE OF INDUSTRIAL AND AGRICULTURAL PRODUCTION

Item	Unit	1949	1959	1959 as a multiple of 1949
Combined gross output value of industry and agriculture	million yuan	**46,610**	**220,800**	5.3
Gross output value of industry	do	14,020	147,000	11.7
Gross output value of agriculture	do	32,590	73,800	2.5
Steel	thousand tons	158	12,000	75.9
Coal	do	32,430	335,000	10.3
Electric power	million kwh.	4,310	39,000	9.1
Metal-cutting machine tools	number	1,582	60,000	37.9
Electric generators	thousand kw.	—	1,800	—
Cotton yarn	thousand bales[1]	1,800	8,200	4.5
Paper	thousand tons	228	2,000	8.8
Grains	million catties	216,200	550,000	2.5
Cotton	thousand *tan*	8,890	46,200	5.2

Note: The first three items are calculated in terms of 1952 constant prices for the year 1949 and in terms of 1957 constant prices for 1959. The absolute figures for 1949 and 1959 for these items are therefore not directly comparable, and the figures in the last column, i.e. 5.3, 11.7 and 2.5 are derived by multiplying the corresponding index numbers.

[1] The weight of one bale of cotton yarn is 181.44 kg. or 400 lb.

[15]

COMBINED GROSS OUTPUT VALUE OF INDUSTRY AND AGRICULTURE (I)

(million yuan)

	Combined gross output value of ind. and agr.	Gross output value of ind.		Gross output value of agr.[1]
		Total	Of which: handicrafts	
(At 1952 prices)				
1949	46,610	14,020	3,240	32,590
1950	57,480	19,120	5,060	38,360
1951	68,320	26,350	6,140	41,970
1952	82,720	34,330	7,310	48,390
1953	94,610	44,700	9,120	49,910
1954	103,540	51,970	10,460	51,570
1955	110,410	54,870	10,120	55,540
1956	128,650	70,360	11,700	58,290
1957	138,740	78,390	13,370	60,350
(At 1957 prices)				
1957	124,100	70,400	—	53,700
1958	184,100	117,000	—	67,100
1959[2]	220,800	147,000	—	73,800

[1]The gross output value of agriculture covers agriculture, forestry, animal husbandry, agricultural side-occupations and fishery (exclusive of fishing by mechanical means). Handicrafts consumed at the rural source of production and preliminary processing of agricultural products are included in the gross output value of agriculture for 1949-1957, but excluded for subsequent years.
[2]Planned.

COMBINED GROSS OUTPUT VALUE OF INDUSTRY AND AGRICULTURE (II)

(percentage distribution)

	Gross output value of industry		Gross output value of agriculture
	Total	Of which: handicrafts	
1949	30.1	6.9	69.9
1950	33.3	8.9	66.7
1951	38.6	9.0	61.4
1952	41.5	8.8	58.5
1953	47.2	9.6	52.8
1954	50.2	10.1	49.8
1955	49.7	9.2	50.3
1956	54.7	9.1	45.3
1957	56.5	9.6	43.5
1958	63.6	—	36.4
1959[1]	66.6	—	33.4

[1]Planned.

COMBINED GROSS OUTPUT VALUE OF INDUSTRY AND AGRICULTURE (III)

(index numbers, preceding year = 100)

	Combined gross output value of ind. and agr.	Gross output value of ind.		Gross output value of agr.
		Total	Of which: handicrafts	
1950	123.3	136.4	156.4	117.7
1951	118.9	137.9	121.3	109.4
1952	121.1	130.3	119.1	115.3
1953	114.4	130.2	124.7	103.1
1954	109.4	116.3	114.7	103.3
1955	106.6	105.6	96.8	107.7
1956	116.5	128.2	115.6	104.9
1957	107.8	111.4	114.2	103.5
1958	148.0	166.2	—	125.0
1959[1]	120.0	125.6	—	110.0

[1]Planned.

[18]

COMBINED GROSS OUTPUT VALUE OF INDUSTRY AND AGRICULTURE (IV)

(index numbers)

	Combined gross output value of ind. and agr.	Gross output value of ind.		Gross output value of agr.
		Total	Of which: handicrafts	
1952 (1949=100)	177.5	244.9	225.9	148.5
1957 (1952=100)	167.7	228.4	182.8	124.7
1958 (1949=100)	440.4	929.4	—	231.4
1959 (1949=100)	529.4	1,170.0	—	254.5
(percentage)				
Average annual increase 1950-1952	21.1	34.8	31.2	14.1
Average annual increase 1953-1957	10.9	18.0	12.8	4.5
Average annual increase 1950-1958	17.9	28.1	—	9.8
Average annual increase 1950-1959[1]	18.1	27.9	—	9.8

[1]The figures for 1959 are planned.

INCREASE OF NATIONAL INCOME

(percentage)

	1949=100	1952=100	Preceding year=100
1950	118.6	—	118.6
1951	138.8	—	117.0
1952	169.7	100.0	122.3
1953	193.4	114.0	114.0
1954	204.4	120.4	105.7
1955	217.8	128.3	106.5
1956	248.3	146.3	114.0
1957	259.7	153.0	104.6
1958[1]	348.0	205.0	134.0

[1]Preliminary.

STATE REVENUES (I)

(million yuan)

	Total	Taxes	Revenue from state-owned enterprises and under-takings	Credits and insurance	Other
1950	6,520	4,900	870	330	420
1951	12,960	8,110	3,050	570	1,230
1952	17,560	9,770	5,730	190	1,870
1953	21,760	11,970	7,670	490	1,630
1954	26,230	13,220	9,960	1,790	1,260
1955	27,200	12,750	11,190	2,360	900
1956	28,740	14,090	13,430	720	500
1957	31,020	15,490	14,420	700	410
1958	41,860	18,730	22,020	800	310

Note: Data do not include carry-overs from the preceding year.

STATE REVENUES (II)

	Taxes	Revenue from state-owned enterprises and undertakings	Credits and insurance	Other
1950	75.1	13.4	5.0	6.5
1951	62.6	23.5	4.4	9.5
1952	55.6	32.6	1.1	10.7
1953	55.0	35.2	2.3	7.5
1954	50.4	38.0	6.8	4.8
1955	46.9	41.1	8.7	3.3
1956	49.0	46.7	2.5	1.8
1957	49.9	46.5	2.3	1.3
1958	44.8	52.6	1.9	0.7

STATE EXPENDITURES (I)

(million yuan)

	Total	Economic construction	Social, cultural, & educational	National defence	Government administration	Other
1950	6,810	1,740	750	2,830	1,310	180
1951	11,900	3,510	1,340	5,060	1,750	240
1952	16,790	7,630	2,280	4,370	1,730	780
1953	21,490	8,650	3,360	5,680	2,120	1,680
1954	24,630	12,360	3,460	5,810	2,160	840
1955	26,920	13,760	3,190	6,500	2,150	1,320
1956	30,580	15,910	4,600	6,120	2,660	1,290
1957	29,020	14,910	4,640	5,510	2,270	1,690
1958	40,960	26,270	4,350	5,000	2,270	3,070

Note: The years 1950-1957 do not include additional appropriations for bank loans.

[23]

STATE EXPENDITURES (II)

(percentage distribution)

	Economic construction	Social, cultural, & educational	National defence	Government administration	Other
1950	25.5	11.1	41.5	19.3	2.6
1951	29.5	11.3	42.5	14.7	2.0
1952	45.4	13.6	26.0	10.3	4.7
1953	40.2	15.7	26.4	9.9	7.8
1954	50.2	14.1	23.6	8.7	3.4
1955	51.1	11.9	24.1	8.0	4.9
1956	52.1	15.0	20.0	8.7	4.2
1957	51.4	16.0	19.0	7.8	5.8
1958	64.1	10.6	12.2	5.6	7.5

INDEX NUMBERS OF STATE REVENUES AND EXPENDITURES

	Revenues	Expenditures
1952 (1950=100)	269.4	246.6
1957 (1952=100)	176.6	172.9
1957 (1950=100)	475.8	426.4
1958 (1950=100)	642.2	601.7

II. THE GREAT VICTORY OF THE SOCIALIST REVOLUTION AND THE PEOPLE'S COMMUNE MOVEMENT

The founding of the People's Republic of China in 1949 marked the basic end of the democratic revolution and the beginning of the socialist revolution in China. Early in the decade the Chinese people completed the historic task of the democratic revolution and won the great victory of the socialist revolution.

The land reform which was carried out in the early stages after the founding of the Republic was a revolutionary change of historic significance. As is known to everyone, the system of landownership in old China was extremely irrational. Landlords and rich peasants, who constituted less than 10 per cent of the rural population, owned over 70 per cent of all the cultivated land. They ruthlessly exploited the peasants. On the other hand, the farm labourers, poor peasants and middle peasants, who accounted for over 90 per cent of the rural population, owned less than 30 per cent of the cultivated land. They toiled the whole year round but could not earn enough for food or clothing. This was the root cause of the centuries-old poverty and backwardness of China.

The confiscation of the land of the landlord class for distribution to the landless or land-poor peasants and the transformation of the landownership system of feudal exploitation into a system of peasant landownership were the basic contents of China's new democratic revolution. Before liberation land reform had already been completed, in the main, in the revolutionary bases and liberated areas led by the Communist Party of China. Following the founding of the People's Republic of China the broad masses of the peasants were immediately organized to carry out a nation-wide, thorough, land reform movement. Within the brief time of three years this historic task was brought to a successful end. By 1952 about 300 million landless or land-poor peasants received about 700 million *mou* of land free of cost and a great number of draught animals, farm implements, houses, etc. Moreover, these peasants no longer had to pay the exorbitant rent to the landlords, which had amounted to an annual total of 70,000 million catties of grain. The feudal system of exploitation in China which had lasted for several thousands of years, was thoroughly eliminated.

By 1952, when the rehabilitation of the national economy and the land reform were successfully completed, the socialist state economy had already grown tremendously. But non-socialist economic elements still existed on a large scale in the national economy as a whole. In agriculture, individual small-scale farming still predominated. In industrial production and commerce the capitalist economy still accounted for a heavy percentage. Had these conditions not been changed drastically it would have been impossible to establish a socialist system in China quickly nor would it have been possible for the country to advance on the path of prosperity and strength.

To overcome the backwardness of China's national economy and speed up the socialist transformation and socialist construction, the Central Committee of the Communist Party of China formulated the well-timed general line for the period of transition from capitalism to socialism when the rehabilitation of the national economy was nearing completion. Under the brilliant guidance of the Party's general line the Chinese people, simultaneously with their planned, large-scale socialist construction, swiftly completed the socialist transformation of agriculture, handicrafts and capitalist industry and commerce.

Following the land reform the Chinese peasants, led by the Communist Party, immediately set up mutual-aid organizations which contained rudiments of socialism. In 1952, 40 per cent of the country's total peasant households belonged to mutual-aid teams, and in 1954 they increased to 58 per cent. Simultaneous with the swift growth of the mutual-aid teams, the peasants started to organize semi-socialist agricultural producers' co-operatives characterized by the pooling of land as shares and a single management. In 1952 there were only about 3,600 agricultural producers' co-operatives, but since these co-operatives proved to have advantages over the mutual-aid teams they grew rapidly. By the first half of 1955 their number increased to 670,000, embracing some 17 million peasant households. In July 1955 Chairman Mao Tse-tung delivered his well-known report *The Question of Agricultural Co-operation*. Based on this report the Central Committee of the Chinese Communist Party adopted the "Decisions on the Question of Agricultural Co-operation" in October of the same year. Under the inspiration of these historically significant documents the peasant masses showed unprecedented socialist enthusiasm. As a result, a high tide of socialist co-operation on a magnificent scale appeared in the second half of 1955. By 1956 agricultural co-operation was in the main completed in China. By the end of 1956, 120 million peasant households, or 96 per cent of all the peasant households in China had joined co-operatives. More than 100 million of them, or 88 per cent, joined the advanced agricultural producers' co-operatives. This showed that the socialist transformation of agriculture was basically completed throughout the length and breadth of China, a social change of profound historic significance which paved the way for the rapid growth of China's productive forces in the countryside.

Under the impetus of the high tide of agricultural co-operation the organization of individual handicraftsmen into co-operatives was also completed in the main in 1956. By the end of 1956 the number of handicraft co-operatives exceeded

100,000, embracing over 6,000,000 handicraftsmen, or 92 per cent of the total number of handicraftsmen in China. At the same time the socialist transformation of the individual economy of the small merchants and pedlars was also in 'the main completed in 1956 through co-operatives.

In dealing with the capitalist industry and commerce the state has carried out the policy of utilization, restriction and transformation — to use the positive side of capitalist industry and commerce which is beneficial to the national welfare and the people's livelihood, while restricting its negative side which is not beneficial to the national welfare and the people's livelihood. This was done mainly through two forms of state capitalism. Briefly speaking, the initial form of state capitalism was to supply private capitalist industries with raw materials and to place orders with them for processing and manufacturing goods. As to private capitalist commercial enterprises, they were allowed to serve as retail distributors or commission agents for the state. The higher form of state capitalism was to place private capitalist enterprises under joint state-private management. The carrying out of these measures step by step transformed capitalist ownership of the means of production to socialist ownership by the whole people. In 1952, 56 per cent of the gross output value of capitalist industry was produced by enterprises under the initial form of state capitalism, i.e. processing goods for the state and executing state orders. In 1952, only five per cent of China's gross output value of industry (exclusive of handicrafts) came from joint state-private industrial enterprises. By 1955, 81.7 per cent of the gross output value of capitalist industry was produced by processing goods for the state and executing state orders, while the gross output value of joint state-private industrial enterprises rose to 16.1 per cent of the gross output value of industry (exclusive of handicrafts) as a whole.

State capitalist commerce did not make marked growth until after 1954. In the latter half of 1953 the state started to introduce planned purchase and distribution of grain. In 1954 cotton cloth was also put under planned purchase and distribution. As a result, many of the capitalist commercial enterprises became state authorized dealers or distributing agents. At the same time, since the sources of all principal commodities were in the hands of state commerce, the state capitalist commerce under various forms developed rapidly. In 1954 the state capitalist share of trade (including the authorized dealers and distributing agents) and co-operative trade in the national total of retail sales was 5.4 per cent. In 1955 it rose to 14.6 per cent.

In the second half of 1955, along with the high tide of agricultural co-operation throughout the nation the socialist transformation of capitalist industry and commerce also entered a new stage. At the beginning of 1956 there was a nation-wide high tide for the conversion of capitalist enterprises into joint state-private enterprises by whole trades. Tens of thousands of capitalists beat gongs and sounded drums in the streets and decorated their shops with lanterns and festoons to welcome this high tide of transformation. By the end of 1956 some 70,000 private industrial establishments came under joint state-private management. The gross output value of these enterprises accounted for 99.6 per cent of the total produced by the former private establishments in industry. In commerce, 1,990,000 shops, large, medium-sized and small, came under joint state-private operation, became co-operative shops and teams or merged with state trading enterprises. These shops employed about 85 per cent of the total number of employees of the former private commercial enterprises. This showed that the socialist transformation of capitalist industry and commerce was practically completed.

Following the successful completion of the socialist transformation of agriculture, handicrafts and capitalist industry and commerce, a fundamental change took place in the economic structure of Chinese society. The socialist sector of the economy was overwhelmingly predominant in the national economy as a whole. The few figures below suffice to show this profound change. Compared with 1952, the percentage increases in the national income by economic sector for 1956 were as follows: the state sector increased from 19.1 per cent to 32.2 per cent; the co-operative sector increased from 1.5 per cent to 53.4 per cent; joint state-private sector jumped from 0.7 per cent to 7.3 per cent. The sector of individual ownership declined from 71.8 per cent to 7.1 per cent and the capitalist sector decreased from 6.9 per cent to less than 0.1 per cent.

Immediately after the great victory of the socialist revolution on the economic front (i.e. the change of ownership of the means of production), in 1957 all the Chinese people, led by the Communist Party, carried out a militant rectification campaign and a struggle against bourgeois rightists, and won a signal victory of the socialist revolution on the political and ideological fronts. The victories on the economic, political and ideological fronts have further consolidated China's socialist political and economic systems and enhanced the working people's initiative and creativeness in building socialism, which in turn promoted the speedy development of the national economy.

In 1958 a big leap forward unparalleled in Chinese history took place in the development of China's national economy. In the course of the big leap forward in 1958, the Chinese people came up with a great creation in social organization — the people's commune, established in response to the demands of the broad masses of peasants throughout the country. Beginning in the summer of 1958, in a few months more than 740,000 agricultural co-operatives were merged and reorganized into over 26,000 large-scale people's communes in which industry, agriculture, trade, education and military affairs were combined and government administration and commune management were merged. The communes embrace 120 million peasant households, or over 99 per cent of the total peasant families of all the nationalities in China.

The emergence of the people's communes is not accidental. They are a product of China's economic and political development and a result of the socialist rectification campaign of the Chinese Communist Party, a result of the general line for building socialism and the big leap in socialist construction in 1958. The form of organization of the people's commune is extremely significant in the social and economic development of China. The establishment of the people's communes gave a great impetus to the big leap in industry and agriculture. In 1958 grain output in China increased 130,000 million catties over the 1957 figure, more than double the total increase during the First Five-Year Plan period which amounted to 61,200 million catties. The cotton output in 1958 increased 9.2 million *tan* over the 1957 figure, or 1.4 times the total cotton increase of 6.73 million *tan* during the First Five-Year Plan period. The summer harvest in 1959 was the first one after the establishment of the people's communes. In spite of the serious natural calamities during the spring and summer of that year the total yields of summer crops of wheat, coarse grains and early rice were still bigger than the extraordinary bumper harvest of 1958. This was due to the fact that the people's communes, after the check-up and consolidation, have further enhanced the peasants' initiative.

In the course of the big leap of 1958 the people's communes, by employing indigenous methods as well as a combination of modern and indigenous methods, set up a number of small iron smelting mills, coal mines, power plants, cement works, fertilizer plants, workshops for producing and repairing farming implements and food processing plants. These small industrial enterprises were further strengthened and improved after the check-up. By the first half of 1959, the industrial units operated by the people's communes numbered more than 700,000 with a gross output value of 7,100 million yuan. This represented about 10 per cent of the gross output value of industry in the country in the corresponding period. Tremendous increases were made in the output of many kinds of products.

After the establishment of people's communes, there was a remarkable development of construction in various fields and a growth in public welfare works. In 1958 the people's communes built more than 1,200 big and medium-sized reservoirs and countless small ones. They also organized huge labour forces to help with railway construction and transport work, thus successfully fulfilling the tremendous task of short-distance transport for farm products and iron and steel production. By the end of 1958 the rural areas had 3,400,000 community dining-rooms, more than 3,400,000 nurseries and kindergartens, 150,000 homes of the respect for the aged, approximately 60,000 cultural halls and stations, 500,000 clubs and more than 180,000 amateur dramatic groups.

The foregoing facts show that the people's communes are the best form of organization for accelerating the tempo of China's socialist construction, for transforming socialist collective ownership into socialist ownership by the whole people in the countryside and for the transition from socialism to communism in the future.

THOROUGH CARRYING OUT OF THE LAND REFORM

1. The changes in the number of *mou* owned by various classes prior to and after the land reform movement: In old China the system of landownership in the countryside was extremely irrational. Landlords and rich peasants, who constituted less than 10 per cent of the rural population, possessed more than 70 per cent of the total arable land. Poor peasants, farm labourers and middle peasants who made up over 90 per cent of the population, possessed less than 30 per cent of the total arable land. After the land reform the poor peasants and middle peasants possessed more than 90 per cent of the total arable land, while the former landlords and rich peasants possessed about 8 per cent of the total arable land.

2. After the completion of the land reform over 300 million peasants who owned little or no land received 700 million *mou* of arable land and other means of production free of charge. In addition, they no longer had to pay the exorbitant rent to the landlords which formerly amounted to 70,000 million catties of grain each year.

AGRICULTURAL CO-OPERATION (I)

(thousand households)

	No. of peasant households in mutual-aid and co-operative organizations	No. of peasant households in agricultural producers' co-operatives			No. of peasant households in mutual-aid teams
		Total	Advanced	Elementary	
1950	11,313	0.219	0.032	0.187	11,313
1951	21,002	1.618	0.030	1.588	21,000
1952	45,423	59	2	57	45,364
1953	45,912	275	2	273	45,637
1954	70,775	2,297	12	2,285	68,478
1955	77,310	16,921	40	16,881	60,389
1956	117,829	117,829	107,422	10,407	—

AGRICULTURAL CO-OPERATION (II)

(percentage)

	Percentage of peasant households in mutual-aid and co-operative organizations to total no. of peasant households	Agricultural producers' co-operatives			Mutual-aid teams
		Total	Advanced	Elementary	
1950	10.7	...	...	...	10.7
1951	19.2	...	...	...	19.2
1952	40.0	0.1	...	0.1	39.9
1953	39.5	0.2	...	0.2	39.3
1954	60.3	2.0	...	2.0	58.3
1955	64.9	14.2	...	14.2	50.7
1956	96.3	96.3	87.8	8.5	—

HANDICRAFT CO-OPERATION

	Number of persons engaged in: (thousands)			Percentage distribution	
	Total	Co-operative handicrafts	Individual handicrafts	Co-operative handicrafts	Individual handicrafts
1952	7,364	228	7,136	3.1	96.9
1953	7,789	301	7,488	3.9	96.1
1954	8,910	1,213	7,697	13.6	86.4
1955	8,202	2,206	5,996	26.9	73.1
1956	6,583	6,039	544	91.7	8.3

Notes: 1. In 1955 and 1956 the number of handicraftsmen decreased because in the course of forming co-operatives some of the handicraftsmen in the cities were absorbed by the industrial enterprises, while in the countryside some of the handicraftsmen joined the agricultural producers' co-operatives.
2. The figure for co-op handicraftsmen in 1956 covers more than 1,000,000 handicraftsmen belonging to fishing and salt co-ops.

RAPID GROWTH OF SOCIALIST INDUSTRY

	Gross output value (million yuan)	Index numbers (1949=100)
At 1952 prices		
1949	3,730	100.0
1950	6,360	170.4
1951	9,290	248.8
1952	15,120	405.1
1953	20,450	548.0
1954	26,090	698.8
1955	30,290	811.6
1956	39,520	1,060.0
1957	44,350	1,190.0
At 1957 prices		
1957	39,470	—
1958	81,290	2,450.0

SOCIALIST TRANSFORMATION OF CAPITALIST INDUSTRY

(percentage distribution of gross output value of industry, excluding handicrafts)

	Socialist industry	State-capitalist industry	Of which:		Capitalist industry (that part produced and marketed by itself)
			Joint state-private enterprises	Privately-owned enterprises executing orders and processing goods for the state	
1949	34.7	9.5	2.0	7.5	55.8
1950	45.3	17.8	2.9	14.9	36.9
1951	45.9	25.4	4.0	21.4	28.7
1952	56.0	26.9	5.0	21.9	17.1
1953	57.5	28.5	5.7	22.8	14.0
1954	62.8	31.9	12.3	19.6	5.3
1955	67.7	29.3	16.1	13.2	3.0
1956	67.5	32.5	32.5	—	...

Notes: In 1956 the capitalist enterprises came under joint state-private operation by whole trades. These enterprises actually were not very different from socialist enterprises except that the capitalists still drew a fixed rate of interest.

In 1956 the gross output value of capitalist industry was less than 0.1 per cent of the gross output value of industry. It was virtually impossible to show this decimal fraction on the above table.

RAPID GROWTH OF SOCIALIST COMMERCE

	Retail sales handled by socialist commerce (million yuan)	Index numbers (1950=100)
1950	1,780	100.0
1951	4,150	233.2
1952	9,000	505.6
1953	13,790	774.7
1954	21,750	1,220.0
1955	21,840	1,230.0
1956	26,260	1,480.0
1957	26,220	1,470.0
1958	36,000	2,020.0

SOCIALIST TRANSFORMATION OF PRIVATE COMMERCE

(percentage distribution of retail sales)

	Socialist commerce	State-capitalist and co-operative commerce	Private commerce
1950	14.9	0.1	85.0
1951	24.4	0.1	75.5
1952	42.6	0.2	57.2
1953	49.7	0.4	49.9
1954	69.0	5.4	25.6
1955	67.6	14.6	17.8
1956	68.3	27.5	4.2
1957	65.7	31.6	2.7

SOCIALIST TRANSFORMATION OF PRIVATE TRANSPORT ENTERPRISES

(percentage distribution of freight turnover)

	State enterprises	Joint state-private enterprises	Private enterprises
1949	88.5	...	11.5
1950	95.3	...	4.7
1951	94.7	...	5.3
1952	95.8	0.7	3.5
1953	95.8	1.3	2.9
1954	95.3	3.1	1.6
1955	94.8	4.6	0.6
1956	99.3	0.7	—
1957	99.7	0.3	—

Note: This table does not include the freight turnover of wooden junks, animal-drawn carts, wheelbarrows and other vehicles that are not mechanically operated.

PREDOMINANT POSITION OF THE SOCIALIST SECTOR IN THE NATIONAL ECONOMY

(percentage distribution of national income)

	State-owned economy	Co-operative economy	Joint state-private economy	Capitalist economy	Individual economy
1952	19.1	1.5	0.7	6.9	71.8
1953	23.9	2.5	0.9	7.9	64.8
1954	26.8	4.8	2.1	5.3	61.0
1955	28.0	14.1	2.8	3.5	51.6
1956	32.2	53.4	7.3	...	7.1
1957	33.2	56.4	7.6	...	2.8

THE GREAT VICTORY OF THE PEOPLE'S COMMUNES IN THE COUNTRYSIDE (1958)

	End of August	Early September	Mid September	Late September	End of December
No. of people's communes	8,730	12,824	16,989	26,425	26,578
No. of peasant households in people's communes (thousands)	37,780	59,790	81,220	121,940	123,250
Percentage of peasant households in people's communes to total no. of peasant households	30.4	48.1	65.3	98.0	99.1
Average no. of households in each commune	4,328	4,662	4,781	4,614	4,637

THE GREAT ACHIEVEMENTS OF THE PEOPLE'S COMMUNES IN THE COUNTRYSIDE

1. Bumper harvests

   The grain output in 1958 increased 130,000 million catties over 1957. The total increase of grain output during the First Five-Year Plan period was 61,200 million catties.

   In 1958 the cotton output increased 9,200,000 *tan* over 1957. The total increase of cotton output during the First Five-Year Plan period was 6,730,000 *tan*.

2. Establishment of industrial enterprises

   By the end of June 1959 the people's communes had established about 700,000 industrial production units. In the first half of 1959 the gross output value of industry of the people's communes reached 7,100 million yuan, representing about 10 per cent of the nation's gross output value of industry.

3. Expansion of welfare services

   Number of welfare facilities existing as of end of 1958:

   Community dining-rooms 3,400,000

   Nurseries and kindergartens . . . . . . over 3,400,000

   Homes of respect for the aged 150,000

   Cultural halls and stations approximately . . . 60,000

   Clubs   500,000

   Amateur dramatic groups . . . . over 180,000

III. THE EXPANSION OF CAPITAL CONSTRUCTION

Socialist revolution and socialist construction in China are interrelated and accelerate each other. As the former scores rapid successes, the latter shows brilliant achievements.

The poverty and ignorance of old China left an extremely difficult but important task for the liberated Chinese people. They had to rapidly change the backwardness of China's national economy in order to make the country rich and strong and bring happiness to the people. China, a backward agricultural country, had to be gradually turned into a great socialist country with a highly developed modern industry, modern agriculture and modern science and culture. In the execution of this great task it was necessary, apart from making full use of the existing productive equipment and developing its potential, to carry out new large-scale capital construction, set up new industrial branches, especially those of heavy industry, provide the various departments of the national economy with new equipment and technique and build strong socialist material and technological foundations.

After a short period of rehabilitation of the national economy following the founding of the People's Republic, large-scale planned economic construction began in 1953. In the nine years between 1950 and 1958, state investments in capital construction in the economic and cultural departments totalled 89,500 million yuan, of which 7,800 million were for the period of rehabilitation, 55,000 million for the period of the First Five-Year Plan and 26,700 million for the year 1958. The average annual investment during the First Five-Year Plan period exceeded the total investment during the rehabilitation period, while the investment in the single year of 1958 was close to 50 per cent of the total investment for the First Five-Year Plan period.

The central task in China's transitional period is to carry out socialist industrialization, and the basic policy for socialist construction is to give priority to the development of heavy industry. Of the more than 86,000 million yuan the state invested in capital construction from 1952 to 1958, 51.1 per cent was for industrial construction, of which 43.8 per cent was for heavy industry. The balance was divided as follows: 8.6 per cent for agriculture, forestry and water conservancy, 15.3 per cent for communications, transport, post and telecommunications, 9 per cent for cultural, educational and public health work and urban public utilities, and 16 per cent for other construction.

The state paid great attention to economic construction and cultural development in the areas inhabited by the national minorities. In the nine years between 1950 and 1958, the state invested 7,160 million yuan in capital construction in these areas, constituting 8 per cent of the total state investment in the same period.

The huge investment in capital construction provided a reliable material and technical guarantee for the high-speed development of China's national economy. In the nine years from 1950 to 1958, the new fixed assets in the whole country amounted to 71,900 million yuan, constituting 80.3 per cent of the total investment in capital construction during this period. Of this figure the new fixed assets in industry amounted to 34,360 million yuan, constituting 76 per cent of the total investment in industrial capital construction. Such new fixed assets in industry during the nine years were 2.7 times the total fixed assets in industry that old China accumulated over a period of 100 years.

Between 1950 and 1958 more than 50,000 factory and mining construction projects were wholly or partially built and went into operation, of which over 1,000 projects were above-norm,[1] large and modern. Of the above-norm factory and mining construction projects completed and already in operation, 113 were constructed with Soviet assistance and more than 40 with the assistance of other fraternal countries — the German Democratic Republic, Czechoslovakia, Poland, Hungary, Rumania and Bulgaria. During the period of the First Five-Year Plan one large factory or mining construction project went into operation every three days on the average, and in 1958 nearly two new projects began to operate each day. The more important of the large, modern factory or mining enterprises completed and functioning in the last ten years are: the iron and steel works at Anshan and Penki, the special steel works in Tayeh, the heavy machine-building works in Shenyang, Fushun, Taiyuan and Wuhan, the electrical machinery works, the boiler works, the measuring instruments and cutting tools plant and the linen mill in Harbin, the steam turbine works and boiler plant in Shanghai, the air compressor plant in Chungking, the motor works in Changchun, the fertilizer plant and dye-making plant in Kirin Province, the thermal power stations in Taiyuan, Kirin and Loyang, the hydro-electric power stations in Kuanting, Shihtsetan, and Ulapo, the Pingan colliery in Fuhsin and the Hsingantai colliery in Hokang, the paper mill at Kiamusze, the sugar mill in Paotow, etc. The Anshan Iron and Steel Works which is capable of producing more than 5 million tons of steel this year, has become one of the ten largest steel works in the world, i.e. with an annual production capacity of more than 3 million tons.

---

[1] To facilitate management and control of major capital construction projects, the state has, in the light of actual conditions in China, set an "investment norm" for every category of capital construction. Any construction project, whether it is new, rebuilt or restored, is classified as "above-norm" or "below-norm" according to whether its invested capital is above or below the "norm" figure. The norm of investment in capital construction for heavy industry ranges from 5 million to 10 million yuan and that for light industry from 3 million to 5 million yuan.

The large-scale industrial construction has brought about conspicuous increases in production capacity. In the period of the First Five-Year Plan alone, the figures for newly increased production capacity of major industrial products (calculated according to the designed annual production capacity) were as follows: electric power (installed capacity), 2,469,000 kilowatts; coal mining, 63,760,000 tons; petroleum, 1,312,000 tons; synthetic oil, 522,000 tons; iron smelting, 3,390,000 tons; steel making, 2,820,000 tons; steel rolling, 1,650,000 tons; lorries, 30,000; synthetic ammonia, 137,000 tons; cement, 2,610,000 tons; machine-made paper, 250,000 tons; machine-processed sugar, 620,000 tons; spindles, 2,010,000; and looms, 55,000. During the great leap forward in 1958, the newly increased production capacity in a large number of industries exceeded the total increase during the First Five-Year Plan period.

Such a rapid increase of production capacity was inconceivable in old China. It took 60 years prior to 1949 to build up a production capacity of only 1,000,000 tons of steel. The capacity for steel making achieved in the past decade in New China is more than eleven times that of old China. The power industry of old China had a history of 70 years, but by 1949 it had a generating capacity of less than 1,900,000 kilowatts. The power-generating capacity achieved in the past ten years in New China is more than three times that of old China. The textile industry increased relatively faster in old China, but in the 60 years from 1890 to 1949, only 5,000,000 spindles were set up, while in New China 3,107,000 spindles were added in the nine years from 1950 to 1958 — 62 per cent of the number set up in 60 years in the old days. Thus, it can be seen what a great leap the socialist system has brought to China's social productive forces.

Large-scale industrial construction has begun to change the backward industry of old China. Not only have existing industries been considerably strengthened, many hitherto nonexistent industries were built capable of producing modern metallurgical equipment, mining equipment, power-generating equipment, aircraft, motor vehicles, tractors, modern machine-tools, high-grade alloy steel metallurgy, important non-ferrous metals, new chemicals, etc.

Large-scale industrial construction has also begun to change the extremely uneven geographical distribution of old China's industries. In those days, industry was mainly concentrated in a few coastal areas, while in the vast hinterland there was practically no modern industry to speak of. Now things are different. In vast remote border regions and the far interior like Inner Mongolia, Shensi, Kansu, Sinkiang, Szechuan, Yunnan, etc., a series of modern factories and mines have been built or are being built. In many old cities and desolate wildernesses long rows of factory buildings and chimneys have appeared. In the deserts and isolated mountains, where human beings rarely came in former days, oil wells and mines have been opened. In 1949 the gross output value of industry of the interior regions was less than a quarter of the gross output value of the country's industry; in 1958 it constituted more than one-third.

Geological prospecting has achieved brilliant successes over the last ten years. In the nine years from 1950 to 1958 drilling work in the whole country exceeded 22,000,000 metres — 130 times the total (about 170,000 metres) done in nearly half a century before liberation. By the end of 1958, the estimates of the newly proved reserves throughout the country included more than 80,000 million tons of coal, more than 8,000 million tons of iron ore and considerable quantities of non-ferrous metals, petroleum and other minerals. During 1958 a nation-wide mass campaign to search for and report on mineral deposits greatly facilitated geological prospecting work. In a number of areas which had been considered lacking in minerals, large quantities of valuable mineral deposits were discovered. The results of geological prospecting and general surveys undertaken by the state and the people on an extensive scale have proved that China is a country with extremely rich mineral resources.

The achievements in the development of agriculture, forestry and water conservancy over the last ten years were also unparalleled in history. To protect agricultural production against the most serious floods and drought, the state, after the founding of the People's Republic, took up water conservancy construction as a vital task in organizing agricultural production. In the seven years between 1952 and 1958 alone, the state spent 4,900 million yuan on water conservancy construction. Of this sum 1,960 million yuan were spent in 1958, 105 times the largest expenditure for water conservancy incurred in any one year by the reactionary Kuomintang government. Many large reservoirs and dams have been built on principal waterways where floods had frequently occurred, such as the large reservoirs at Meishan, Futseling, Hsianghungtien and Motsetan in Anhwei Province; the reservoirs at Nanwan, Poshan, Paisha and Panchiao in Honan Province; the reservoirs at Touho in Hopei Province; the reservoirs at Tahofang in Liaoning Province; the reservoirs at Kuanting, the Ming Tombs and Miyun in Peking; and the reservoirs at Taihangti and Tungpinghu in Shantung Province. In addition, over a dozen large sluice gates were built such as the Sanho dam, the diversion gates and flood regulating gates of the Chingkiang flood diversion project, the Tuchiatai diversion gates, the Tuliuchien River diversion gates, etc. The water conservancy project at the Sanmen Gorge which is the key project in the gigantic engineering undertaking for the permanent control of the Yellow River, began its work in April 1957, and this year it started to check floods. These large water conservancy works play a very important role in preventing floods, storing water, irrigation and power generation. They effectively help develop industrial and agricultural production.

In the past ten years, most of the river embankments have been repaired or reinforced. Permanent control has been virtually put on the rivers which used to cause frequent floods, such as the Huai, the Yi, the Shu, the Yungting, the Taching, the Liao, etc. The state also makes plans for the whole basins of the Yangtse and the Hai Rivers, the Grand Canal and other large and medium-sized rivers. Extensive surveys and investigations of waterways have been conducted and rich and valuable geological and hydrological data were obtained to facilitate the planned development of water conservancy work and permanent control of floods. Simultaneously as the state carried out large-scale water conservancy construction, the broad masses of peasants have undertaken a large number of small-scale irrigation projects on a more extensive scale than they had ever done before. In the nine years between 1950 and 1958 a total of over 70,000 million cubic metres of earth-work and masonry were completed for water conservancy in the whole country. This was equal to the work of excavating 400 Panama Canals or 960 Suez Canals. If such earthwork and masonry could be connected in one line in one cubic metre volume, it would be 1,770 times as long as the equator.

In communications, transport, post and tele-communications, the achievements in the past ten years were also impressive. By the end of 1958 there were 31,193 kilometres of railway lines in operation in China, an increase of 42 per cent over 1949. In the nine years between 1950 and 1958, over 16,500 kilometres of trunk lines, double-track lines, branch lines and special lines for certain establishments were built or rebuilt. Of this figure, 3,564 kilometres of tracks were laid in 1958 alone, double the trackage laid in 1957. The principal new lines are: the 505-kilometre Chengtu-Chungking Railway, a dream of the people of Szechuan in forty years before liberation; the 669-kilometre Paochi-Chengtu Railway, a difficult engineering feat calling for numerous tunnels through high mountains; the Yingtan-Amoy Railway which crosses the mountainous areas of Kiangsi and Fukien; the Tienshui-Lanchow and Paotow-Lanchow Railways over the vast Northwest; the Chining-Erhlien Railway stretching to the People's Republic of Mongolia and the Soviet Union; and the Laipin-Munankuan Railway to the border of the Democratic Republic of Vietnam. Over 1,000 kilometres of tracks have been laid on the Lanchow-Sinkiang Railway which cuts across the Northwest border region, climbs over the Wushao Range 3,000 metres above sea level, and passes vast swamps and alkaline lands. Work has begun on the Szechuan-Kweichow, Neikiang-Kunming, Hunan-Kweichow and Yunnan-Kweichow Railways which traverse the great Southwest. Side by side with the building of new lines, the technical equipment of the existing lines has been supplemented or overhauled. Many double tracks have been laid and traffic capacity expanded. The Yangtse River Bridge at Wuhan, a gigantic engineering project connecting the Peking-Hankow and Canton-Hankow Railways was completed and open to traffic in October 1957, two years ahead of schedule. Thenceforth, the "natural barrier" between the north and south was bridged.

Likewise, the construction of highways has been unprecedented. By the end of 1958, 400,000 kilometres of highways in the country were in use, an increase of five times over 1949. Worthy of special mention is the building of the Sikang-Tibet, Chinghai-Tibet and Sinkiang-Tibet Highways successively opened to traffic some time ago. The extremely difficult and hazardous engineering work done 3,000 metres above sea level would have been an unusual feat anywhere in the world. These highways have brought the Tibetan people closer to the other fraternal nationalities in the country and established closer contact with other regions, thereby increasing economic and cultural contacts. Between the rural districts and medium-sized and small cities many lower grade roads have been built. In 1958, 97 per cent of the county towns could be reached by motor vehicle.

Many inland rivers were dredged, new canals were built and new waterways were opened for navigation in the last ten years. The Grand Canal connects five large waterways, the Hai, the Yellow, the Huai, the Yangtse and the Chientang, but it has been silted up in many places for over 100 years. Dredging and reconstruction work began in Shantung and Kiangsu in 1958 and will continue section by section.

With the rapid progress of economic construction, the state has built a large number of houses for workers and other employees and done much in construction for social amenities and culture. New cities have risen in different parts of the country and old cities have changed their shabby appearance. In the nine years between 1950 and 1958 more than 410,000,000 square metres of floor space were added to the urban buildings throughout the country. In not a few cities the new buildings have greatly exceeded the total of old buildings. Urban public utilities have expanded rapidly. In nine years the length of pipes for running water increased by over 8,100 kilometres, the drainage system was expanded by over 4,000 kilometres and city roads were extended by over 7,600 kilometres.

In the nine years between 1950 and 1958, new school buildings for higher educational institutes increased their floor space by 11,720,000 square metres as a result of state investments in capital construction. This additional building space is 3.5 times as much as all the floor space for higher educational institutes in old China. New buildings for middle schools and normal middle schools increased by 17,720,000 square metres, 3 times as much as all buildings for such schools that existed in old China.

With the speedy progress of socialist construction, the personnel engaged in building work, prospecting and designing has increased as never before. By the end of 1958 the number of workers and other employees in building construction reached 5,336,000, amounting to 5.4 times the number in 1952; the number of workers and other employees in administratively independent prospecting and designing organizations increased 7 times in comparison with the end of 1952. The number of geological prospecting personnel exceeded 420,000 by the end of 1958, 14 times the 1952 figure and 530 times all geological personnel before liberation. As the ranks of

[53]

the workers and other employees in the building industry swelled continuously, their technological equipment inproved and increased and their labour productivity rose conspicuousiy. In 1958 the fixed assets for equipment per building worker increased 2.7 times compared with 1952 and the building workers' labour productivity increased 59 per cent over 1952. The technical level of prospecting, designing and construction has improved greatly. Since 1958 China has been able to make her own designs for the larger and technically more complicated industrial establishments such as an integrated iron and steel works with an annual production capacity of 3,600,000 tons of steel; a colliery capable of producing 3,000,000 tons of coal a year; a hydro-electric power station with a capacity of 1,000,000 kilowatts; a thermal power station with a capacity of 650,000 kilowatts; and a paper mill producing 300 tons daily. In 1958 a much greater number of inventions and innovations in designing and building were introduced by the workers and other employees who had thrown off all the shackles of their old way of thinking and broken away from set traditions and hard and fast rules. In that year, by introducing and popularizing more efficient building methods aimed at achieving greater, quicker, better and more economical results, many important projects went into operation ahead of schedule, saving large sums of money. For example, the blast furnace in the Wuhan Iron and Steel Works with a daily output capacity of 2,000 tons of pig iron, scheduled to be built in two years, was completed and went into operation in 14 months as a result of quick working methods; the large open-hearth furnace in the Anshan Iron and Steel Works with a daily output capacity of 1,000 tons of steel was built in a little more than four months and went into operation, also as a result of using quick working methods. The increase in the number of the personnel in capital construction and the improvement in their working efficiency and technology have created favourable conditions for the speedy development of socialist construction.

INCREASE IN TOTAL INVESTMENT IN CAPITAL CONSTRUCTION

	Total investment (million yuan)	Index numbers		
		Preceding year=100	1950=100	1952=100
Total	**89,540**	—	—	—
Period of Rehabilitation of National Economy				
Total	7,840	—	—	—
1950	1,130	—	100	—
1951	2,350	207	207	—
1952	4,360	186	384	100
First Five-Year Plan Period				
Total	55,000	—	—	—
1953	8,000	184	706	184
1954	9,070	113	799	208
1955	9,300	103	820	214
1956	14,800	159	1,310	340
1957	13,830	93	1,220	317
Second Five-Year Plan Period				
1958	26,700	193	2,350	613

Note: Data include both the investment within the state plan and that outside the state plan.

INCREASE IN INVESTMENT WITHIN STATE PLAN

	Investment within state plan (million yuan)	Index numbers		
		Preceding year=100	1950=100	1952=100
Total	**102,140**	—	—	—
Period of Rehabilitation of National Economy				
Total	6,630	—	—	—
1950	1,040	—	100	—
1951	1,880	180	180	—
1952	3,710	198	356	100
First Five-Year Plan Period				
Total	49,270	—	—	—
1953	6,510	175	625	175
1954	7,500	115	720	202
1955	8,630	115	829	233
1956	13,990	162	1,340	377
1957	12,640	90	1,210	341
Second Five-Year Plan Period				
1958	21,440	170	2,060	578
1959 (planned)	24,800	116	2,380	668

INVESTMENT IN THE DEPARTMENTS OF THE NATIONAL ECONOMY AND CULTURE (I)

(million yuan)

	Total	Industry	Building	Prospecting for natural resources	Agriculture, forestry, water conservancy and meteorology	
					Total	Of which: water conservancy
Total	86,060	44,020	2,510	1,970	7,420	4,920
1952	4,360	1,690	90	70	600	410
First Five-Year Plan Period						
Total	55,000	25,030	2,150	1,430	4,190	2,550
1953	8,000	2,840	360	190	770	480
1954	9,070	3,830	360	290	420	220
1955	9,300	4,300	320	250	620	410
1956	14,800	6,820	650	400	1,190	710
1957	13,830	7,240	460	300	1,190	730
Second Five-Year Plan Period						
1958	26,700	17,300	270	470	2,630	1,960

INVESTMENT IN THE DEPARTMENTS OF THE NATIONAL ECONOMY AND CULTURE (I) (cont'd)

(million yuan)

	Transport, post & tele-communications		Trade	Culture, educa-tion & scientific research	Public health & wel-fare	Urban public utili-ties	Govt. bureau	Other
	Total	Of which: railways						
Total	**13,170**	**8,460**	**2,830**	**4,690**	**820**	**2,190**	**1,180**	**5,260**
1952	760	510	120	280	60	170	20	500
First Five-Year Plan Period								
Total	9,010	5,920	2,140	3,810	650	1,440	970	4,180
1953	1,070	650	270	620	150	250	280	1,200
1954	1,500	950	390	680	150	240	210	1,000
1955	1,760	1,220	350	590	110	220	140	640
1956	2,610	1,760	760	1,000	110	350	160	750
1957	2,070	1,340	370	920	130	380	180	590
Second Five-Year Plan Period								
1958	3,400	2,030	570	600	110	580	190	580

INVESTMENT IN THE DEPARTMENTS OF THE NATIONAL ECONOMY AND CULTURE (II)

(percentage distribution)

	Industry	Building	Prospecting for natural resources	Agriculture, forestry, water conservancy and meteorology		Transport, post & tele-communications	
				Total	Of which: water conservancy	Total	Of which: railways
Total	**51.1**	**2.9**	**2.3**	**8.6**	**5.7**	**15.3**	**9.8**
1952	38.8	2.1	1.6	13.8	9.4	17.5	11.6
First Five-Year Plan Period							
Total	45.5	3.9	2.6	7.6	4.6	16.4	10.8
1953	35.4	4.5	2.4	9.7	6.0	13.4	8.1
1954	42.3	3.9	3.2	4.6	2.5	16.5	10.4
1955	46.2	3.5	2.7	6.7	4.4	19.0	13.2
1956	46.1	4.4	2.7	8.0	4.8	17.7	11.9
1957	52.3	3.3	2.2	8.6	5.3	15.0	9.7
Second Five-Year Plan Period							
1958	64.8	1.0	1.7	9.9	7.3	12.7	7.6

Note: The classifications in this table are functional and not administrative. On an administrative basis, the percentage distribution of total investment actually completed during the First Five-Year Plan would be as follows: industry (including building and geological prospecting) 56 per cent; agriculture, forestry and water conservancy 8.2 per cent; transport, post and tele-communications 18.7 per cent.

INVESTMENT IN THE DEPARTMENTS OF THE NATIONAL ECONOMY AND CULTURE (II) (cont'd)

(percentage distribution)

	Trade	Culture, education & scientific research	Public health & welfare	Urban public utilities	Govt. bureau	Other
Total	**3.3**	**5.5**	**1.0**	**2.5**	**1.4**	**6.1**
1952	2.8	6.4	1.3	3.9	0.4	11.4
First Five-Year Plan Period						
Total	3.9	6.9	1.2	2.6	1.8	7.6
1953	3.4	7.8	1.9	3.1	3.4	15.0
1954	4.3	7.5	1.7	2.6	2.3	11.1
1955	3.7	6.3	1.1	2.4	1.5	6.9
1956	5.1	6.7	0.7	2.4	1.1	5.1
1957	2.7	6.7	0.9	2.8	1.3	4.2
Second Five-Year Plan Period						
1958	2.1	2.3	0.4	2.2	0.7	2.2

INVESTMENT IN HEAVY AND LIGHT INDUSTRY (I)

(absolute figures and percentage distribution)

	Absolute figures (million yuan)			Percentage distribution			Ratio of light to heavy industry
	Industry total	Of which:		Industry total	Of which:		
		Light	Heavy		Light	Heavy	
Total	**44,020**	**6,330**	**37,690**	**100**	**14.4**	**85.6**	**1:6.0**
1952	1,690	410	1,280	100	24.0	76.0	1:3.2
First Five-Year Plan Period							
Total	25,030	3,740	21,290	100	15.0	85.0	1:5.7
1953	2,840	500	2,340	100	17.6	82.4	1:4.7
1954	3,830	670	3,160	100	17.6	82.4	1:4.7
1955	4,300	530	3,770	100	12.3	87.7	1:7.1
1956	6,820	940	5,880	100	13.8	86.2	1:6.2
1957	7,240	1,100	6,140	100	15.2	84.8	1:5.6
Second Five-Year Plan Period							
1958	17,300	2,180	15,120	100	12.6	87.4	1:6.9

Note: In the First Five-Year Plan period, investments within the state plan in light industry constituted 12.6 per cent and those in heavy industry 87.4 per cent.

INVESTMENT IN HEAVY AND LIGHT INDUSTRY (II)

(index numbers)

	Preceding year=100		1952=100	
	Light industry	Heavy industry	Light industry	Heavy industry
1953	123	182	123	182
1954	135	136	166	246
1955	78	119	130	293
1956	179	156	233	458
1957	117	104	273	478
1958	197	246	538	1,180

INVESTMENT IN CAPITAL CONSTRUCTION IN NATIONAL MINORITY AREAS

	Total (million yuan)	Percentage to total national investment	Index numbers	
			Preceding year=100	1952=100
Total	**7,160**	**8.0**	—	—
Period of Rehabilitation of National Economy				
Total	560	7.1	—	—
First Five-Year Plan Period				
Total	3,930	7.1	—	—
1953	390	4.9	121.2	121.2
1954	570	6.2	143.3	173.6
1955	660	7.1	116.8	202.8
1956	1,160	7.8	175.5	355.8
1957	1,150	8.3	99.1	352.8
Second Five-Year Plan Period				
1958	2,670	10.0	232.4	819.9

NEW FIXED ASSETS (I)

(absolute figures and percentage distribution)

	Absolute figures (million yuan)			Percentage distribution		
		Of which:			Of which:	
	Total	Produc-tive	Non-pro-ductive	Total	Produc-tive	Non-pro-ductive
Total	**69,100**	**51,170**	**17,930**	**100**	**74**	**26**
1952	3,110	1,950	1,160	100	63	37
First Five-Year Plan Period						
Total	46,030	32,060	13,970	100	70	30
1953	6,560	3,750	2,810	100	57	43
1954	7,370	4,610	2,760	100	63	37
1955	8,020	5,780	2,240	100	72	28
1956	11,160	8,240	2,920	100	74	26
1957	12,920	9,680	3,240	100	75	25
Second Five-Year Plan Period						
1958	19,960	17,160	2,800	100	86	14

Notes: 1. Productive investment in fixed assets include: factory buildings, machinery and equipment used for production purposes, railways, highways, harbours, wharves and other transport facilities, warehouses for commercial and banking undertakings, etc. Non-productive investment in fixed assets include expenditures for the people's material and cultural life such as housing, school buildings, hospitals, nurseries, cinemas and theatres, clubs, dining-halls and offices for government and people's organizations.

2. New fixed assets within the state plan added during the First Five-Year Plan period amounted to 41,100 million yuan. The balance was outside the state plan.

NEW FIXED ASSETS (II)

(index numbers)

	Preceding year=100		1952=100	
	Productive fixed assets	Non-productive fixed assets	Productive fixed assets	Non-productive fixed assets
1953	192	243	192	243
1954	123	98	236	237
1955	125	81	296	193
1956	143	131	422	252
1957	117	111	495	280
1958	177	86	878	241

NEW INDUSTRIAL FIXED ASSETS

	Absolute figures (million yuan)		Percentage of new fixed industrial assets to total new fixed assets
	New fixed assets total	Of which: new fixed industrial assets	
Total	**71,890**	**34,360**	**47.8**
Period of Rehabilitation of National Economy			
Total	5,900	1,930	32.7
1950	1,010	300	29.7
1951	1,780	500	28.1
1952	3,110	1,130	36.3
First Five-Year Plan Period			
Total	46,030	20,060	43.6
1953	6,560	2,340	35.7
1954	7,370	2,820	38.3
1955	8,020	3,530	44.0
1956	11,160	4,900	43.9
1957	12,920	6,470	50.1
Second Five-Year Plan Period			
1958	19,960	12,370	62.0

Note: The classifications in this table are functional. On an administrative basis, new fixed industrial assets during the First Five-Year Plan period total 21,400 million yuan.

NUMBER OF MAJOR FACTORY AND MINING PROJECTS COMPLETED OR UNDER CONSTRUCTION
(1953-1958)

	No. of projects completed or under construction	Of which: no. of projects wholly or partially in operation
Total	**2,056**	**1,037**
Of which:		
Coal industry	376	179
Electric power industry	268	154
Petroleum industry	28	17
Ferrous metals industry	117	68
Chemical industry	116	54
Building materials industry	103	37
Metal processing industry	489	215
Textile industry	120	74
Paper industry	47	21
Food industry	103	49

Note: A project on which construction continues for several years and which goes into operation by stages is counted only once in this table.

PRINCIPAL NEW RESERVOIRS
(1950-1958)

Reservoir	Location	Date completed	Storage capacity (million cubic metres)
Kuanting Reservoir	Peking	May 1954	2,270
Futseling Reservoir	Huoshan, Anhwei	October 1954	582
Poshan Reservoir	Chuehshan, Honan	December 1954	292
Nanwan Reservoir	Hsinyang, Honan	December 1955	932
Meishan Reservoir	Chinchai, Anhwei	April 1956	2,275
Touho Reservoir	Tangshan, Hopei	December 1956	134
Paisha Reservoir	Yuhsien, Honan	August 1957	274
Panchiao Reservoir	Miyang, Honan	August 1957	418
Shihmen Reservoir	Chunghsiang, Hupeh	July 1957	123
Huaijou Reservoir	Peking	July 1958	90
Tahofang Reservoir	Fushun, Liaoning	September 1958	1,970
Taihangti Reservoir	Tsaohsien, Shantung	August 1958	1,230
Tungpinghu Reservoir	Liaocheng, Liangshan, Shantung	October 1958	4,000
Tungchang Reservoir	Fuching, Fukien	December 1958	186
Mokuhu Reservoir	Manass, Sinkiang	December 1958	158
Hsianghungtien Reservoir	Chinchai, Anhwei	December 1958	2,650
Motsetan Reservoir	Huoshan, Anhwei	December 1958	336
Ming Tombs Reservoir	Peking	July 1958	82

LENGTH OF RAILWAY TRACKS LAID

(kilometres)

	Trunk and branch lines					Special purpose lines
	Total	New lines	Restored lines	New double-track lines	Restored double-track lines	
Total	**12,090**	**7,513**	**1,749**	**1,833**	**995**	**4,451**
Period of Rehabilitation of National Economy						
Total	3,062	1,320	1,170	—	572	593
1950	808	97	427	—	284	172
1951	1,021	743	138	—	140	185
1952	1,233	480	605	—	148	236
First Five-Year Plan Period						
Total	6,652	4,861	474	894	423	2,670
1953	706	587	—	14	105	494
1954	1,132	831	—	49	252	283
1955	1,406	1,222	39	87	58	458
1956	2,242	1,747	285	206	4	866
1957	1,166	474	150	538	4	569
Second Five-Year Plan Period						
1958	2,376	1,332	105	939	—	1,188

Note: In addition to the above figures, 4,400 kilometres of narrow-gauge tracks for forest railways were laid between 1950 and 1958.

[69]

PRINCIPAL NEW RAILWAYS
(1950-1958)

Name of railway	Length of tracks laid (kilometres)	Date opened to traffic
Laipin-Munankuan (Kwangsi)	419	October 1951
Chengtu-Chungking (Szechuan)	505	July 1952
Tienshui-Lanchow (Kansu)	354	October 1952
Litang (Kwangsi)-Chankiang (Kwangtung)	315	July 1955
Fengtai (Peking)-Shacheng (Hopei)	101	July 1955
Chining-Erhlien (Inner Mongolia)	337	December 1955
Hsiaoshan-Chuanshan (Chekiang)	140	April 1956
Paochi (Shensi)-Chengtu (Szechuan)	669	July 1956
Yingtan (Kiangsi)-Amoy (Fukien)	733	April 1957
Paotow (Inner Mongolia) Lanchow (Kansu)	991	August 1958
Nanping-Foochow (Fukien)	167	December 1958
Tuyun-Kweiyang (Kweichow)	146	December 1958
The Greater Khingan Mountains Forest Railway	258	1957 (Huder-Kenho and Etulgol-Gangol sections)
The Lesser Khingan Mountains Forest Railway	115	1957 (Yichun-Hsinching section)
Huaijou (Peking)-Chengteh (Hopei)	106	1958 (Shangpancheng-Yingshouyingtse and Huaijou-Miyun sections)
Lanchow (Kansu)-Sinkiang Friendship Line	1,151	October 1958 (up to Kizil Ulson)
Neikiang (Szechuan)-Kunming (Yunnan)	116	October 1958 (Neikiang-Ipin section)

MAJOR NEW BRIDGES
(1950–1958)

Name	Place	Length (metres)
Wuhan Yangtse River Bridge	Hupeh	1,670
Tungkuan Yellow River Bridge (temporary structure)	Shensi	1,070
Hunan-Kweichow Railway Hsiangkiang Bridge	Hunan	844
Shenyang-Shanhaikuan Railway Talingho Bridge	Liaoning	830
Fengtai-Shacheng Railway Yungtingho No. 1 Bridge	Hopei	722
Lunghai Railway Hsinyiho Bridge	Kiangsu	700
Paotow-Lanchow Railway Sanshengkung Yellow River Bridge	Inner Mongolia	683
Peking-Paotow Railway Kueishui Bridge	Hopei	663
Hunan-Kwangsi Railway Liukiang Bridge	Kwangsi	616
Peking-Canton Railway Changho Bridge	Hopei	569
Fengtai-Shacheng Railway Yungtingho No. 8 Bridge	Hopei	526

LENGTH OF NEW AND IMPROVED HIGHWAYS

(kilometres)

	Total	Of which: new highways
Total	**409,017**	**237,249**
Period of Rehabilitation of National Economy		
Total	46,176	3,846
1950	15,463	540
1951	19,545	1,366
1952	11,168	1,940
First Five-Year Plan Period		
Total	152,841	83,403
1953	9,654	2,598
1954	7,164	3,824
1955	8,138	3,579
1956	89,717	55,930
1957	38,168	17,472
Second Five-Year Plan Period		
1958	210,000	150,000

Note: Figures for 1956 and after include lower grade highways.

PRINCIPAL TRUNK HIGHWAYS COMPLETED

Name of highway	Length (kilometres)	Year completed
1. New highways		
Golmo-Sorhol (Chinghai)	544	1952
Yangchieh-Yinmin (Yunnan)	243	1953
Taotangho-Yushu (Chinghai)	723	1953
Sikang-Tibet (from Chinchikuan in Yaan, Szechuan to Lhasa, Tibet)	2,271	1954
Chinghai-Tibet (from Sining, Chinghai to Lhasa, Tibet)	2,100	1954
Haikow-Yulin (Hainan Island, Kwangtung)	297	1954
Taliyuan-Menghai (Yunnan)	675	1954
Chengtu-Ahpa (Szechuan)	506	1954
Yangpachan-Shigatze (Tibet)	247	1954
Shigatze-Pharhi (Tibet)	253	1954
Tunhuang (Kansu)-Golmo (Chinghai)	588	1954
Nata-Paso (Hainan Island, Kwangtung)	126	1954
Hsinyi-Loting section of Canton-Haian Line (Kwangtung)	124	1954
Pengkow-Chuehwei (Fukien)	274	1955
Menghai-Lantsang(Yunnan)	119	1955
Kaiping-Chuangho (Liaoning)	150	1955
Foochow (Fukien)-Wenchow (Chekiang)	446	1956
Haipachuang-Mengting (Yunnan)	574	1956
Yanglin-Huitse (Yunnan)	280	1956

Name of highway	Length (kilometres)	Year completed
Tungyuanpao-Chuangho (Liaoning)	198	1956
Eh-odot-Mangyai (Chinghai)	371	1956
Lenghu-Chalengkou (Chinghai)	130	1956
Odo-Shaliangtse (Chinghai)	150	1956
Moho-Huangkualiang(Chinghai)	757	1956
Tseli-Tajung (Hunan)	111	1956
Mae Tag-Khoshtologai (Sinkiang)	288	1956
Charklik-Cherchen (Sinkiang)	353	1956
Hsinshihchen-Hsichang (Szechuan)	336	1956
Lhasa-Chetang (Tibet)	184	1956
Sinkiang-Tibet (Karghalik, Sinkiang-Gartok, Tibet)	1,210	1957
Tangin-Mangyai (Chinghai)	363	1957
Weifang-Jungcheng (Shantung)	332	1958
Tungngolo-Patang (Szechuan)	406	1958
Taiho (or Santu)-Chinkangshan (Kiangsi)	95	1958
Hungliuyuan-Tunhuang (Kansu)	127	1958

2. Rebuilt highways

Name of highway	Length (kilometres)	Year completed
Shangyao (Kiangsi)-Foochow (Fukien)	488	1952
Kiangshan (Chekiang)-Chienou (Fukien)	280	1954
Nanping-Pengkow (Fukien)	266	1955
Urumchi-Korla-Kashgar (Sinkiang)	1,513	1958

NEW SCHOOL BUILDINGS

(thousand square metres of floor space)

	Total	Institutes of higher learning	Normal middle schools	Middle schools	Primary schools
Total	**33,590**	**11,720**	**2,070**	**15,650**	**4,150**
Period of Rehabilitation of National Economy					
Total	4,640	1,730	510	1,930	470
1950	540	190	90	150	110
1951	1,280	520	120	510	130
1952	2,820	1,020	300	1,270	230
First Five-Year Plan Period					
Total	22,900	8,340	1,410	10,510	2,640
1953	4,220	1,510	480	2,010	220
1954	4,500	1,530	210	2,300	460
1955	3,710	1,330	150	1,460	770
1956	5,040	2,050	300	2,200	490
1957	5,430	1,920	270	2,540	700
Second Five-Year Plan Period					
1958	6,050	1,650	150	3,210	**1,040**

Note: Data exclude newly added floor space for technical middle schools.

[75]

IMPROVEMENT IN DESIGNING TECHNIQUE
(designed plant capacity)

	1952	1957	1958
Coal mining	—	2,400,000 tons a year	3,000,000 tons a year
Hydro-electric power station	12,000 kw.	1,000,000 kw.	1,000,000 kw.
Thermal power station	10,000 kw.	650,000 kw.	650,000 kw.
Iron and steel integrated works	—	1,500,000 tons a year	3,600,000 tons a year
Heavy machine-building works	—	74,000 tons a year	120,000 tons a year
Paper mill	—	120 tons a day	300 tons a day
Sugar mill (sugar-beet)	800 tons processed a day	1,000 tons processed a day	1,000 tons processed a day
(sugar-cane)	1,000 tons processed a day	2,000 tons processed a day	2,000 tons processed a day

GEOLOGICAL PROSPECTING

(thousand metres)

	Drilling		Pit testing
	Total	Of which: mechanical core drilling	
Total	**22,094**	**18,182**	**2,170**
Period of Rehabilitation of National Economy			
Total	496	409	52
1952	355	286	50
First Five-Year Plan Period			
Total	12,898	10,373	1,458
1953	922	744	151
1954	1,479	1,157	222
1955	2,095	1,599	251
1956	4,141	3,270	401
1957	4,261	3,603	433
Second Five-Year Plan Period			
1958	8,700	7,400	660

CONSTRUCTION OF URBAN PUBLIC UTILITIES

	1949	1952	1957	1958
Running water:				
Length of pipes (kilometres)	6,480	8,099	12,570	14,617
Volume of water supplied for the year (million cubic metres)	—	460	950	1,260
Of which: for household use (million cubic metres)	—	250	550	640
Motor buses:				
Number of buses	1,264	2,220	4,445	5,830
Number of passengers carried (million rides)	—	450	1,930	2,220
Trams:				
Number of cars	866	1,049	1,224	1,245
Number of passengers carried (million rides)	—	550	940	890
Trolley buses:				
Number of buses	166	244	493	688
Number of passengers carried (million rides)	—	110	320	390
Length of roads paved (kilometres)	11,084	12,223	17,730	18,698
Length of drainage pipes (kilometres)	6,568	7,070	10,122	11,074

IV. HIGH RATE OF GROWTH OF INDUSTRIAL OUTPUT

Industrialization was a long-cherished dream of the Chinese people. This dream started to become a reality after the founding of the Chinese People's Republic. In the short period of ten years the foundation has already been laid for China's socialist industrialization.

Industry in old China was extremely backward, particularly in respect to the foundation of heavy industry. The output value of modern industry before the anti-Japanese war accounted for only about 10 per cent of the combined gross output value of industry and agriculture. Of the industrial output, the proportion devoted to light industry producing consumer goods amounted to over 70 per cent, while heavy industry manufacturing the means of production constituted less than 30 per cent. Nevertheless, even this small heavy industry was very incomplete. Its various departments, mostly mining and production of raw materials, were not co-ordinated with each other. The machine-building industry was deplorable. The main work was repairing and assembling. The meagre scope of old China's industry and its low technical level were known to the whole world. This situation was a large factor in China's weakness as a state, the poverty of her people and her infinite suffering from imperialist aggression and oppression in the last century.

After the founding of the People's Republic of China, the state quickly restored the industry that had been seriously damaged in the long years of war and launched a large-scale programme for industrial construction with concentration on heavy industry. In this, China achieved tremendous successes and succeeded in laying the foundation for socialist industrialization.

The Chinese people completed the rehabilitation of the national economy in three years. By 1952, the output of the major industrial products had regained or surpassed the highest pre-liberation levels. The magnificent First Five-Year Plan for the Development of the National Economy was launched in 1953. One of its fundamental tasks was to lay a preliminary foundation for the socialist industrialization of the country. This task was victoriously completed in 1957. The year 1958 witnessed an unprecedented great leap forward of the national economy. China's industrial production and construction developed at an unexampled speed, pushing China a big step forward towards industrialization. This unusually rapid rate of growth was brought about under the guidance of the Party's general line for building socialism and the policy of "walking on two legs" — the policy of simultaneous development of industry and agriculture on the basis of giving priority to heavy industry, simultaneous development of heavy and light industry with priority to heavy industry, simultaneous development of industries run by central and local authorities, simultaneous development of large industrial enterprises, medium enterprises and small ones, simultaneous development of modern and indigenous methods of production and the policy of combining centralized leadership with full-scale mass movements.

The gross industrial output value in 1958 amounted to 117,000 million yuan, 66 per cent higher than in 1957 and 9.3 times that of 1949, an average annual growth rate of 28.1 per cent.

The quick expansion of industrial production resulted in a noticeable change in the position of industry in the entire national economy. The proportion of the gross output of industry to the combined gross output value of industry and agriculture was 30.1 per cent in 1949. It rose to 41.5 per cent in 1952 and 63.6 per cent in 1958. If reckoned in net output value, industrial production in 1958 accounted for 44 per cent of the combined net output value of industry and agriculture.

In industrial production, the output of the means of production showed a particularly fast increase. The output value of the means of production reached 67,000 million yuan in 1958. This was 103 per cent higher than in 1957 and nearly 21 times the 1949 figure; an average annual rate of increase of 40 per cent. As a result of its more rapid growth, the proportion of the means of production in the gross output value of industry rose from 26.6 per cent in 1949 to 35.6 per cent in 1952 and 57.3 per cent in 1958.

While priority was given to the development of heavy industry, light industry also grew quickly in the past ten years. The output value of consumer goods totalled 50,000 million yuan in 1958, 34 per cent higher than in 1957 and 5.3 times that of 1949. The average annual rate of increase was 20.2 per cent.

Comparing the output of the major industrial products in 1958 with that of 1949, steel (not including steel produced by indigenous methods) increased 50.6 times, pig iron (not including iron produced by indigenous methods) 37.8 times, coal 8.3 times, electric power 6.4 times, crude petroleum 18.7 times, metal-cutting machine tools 31.6 times, sulphuric acid 18.5 times, soda-ash 7.3 times, caustic soda 18 times, chemical fertilizers (not including ammonium nitrate) 30 times, cotton yarn 3.4 times, cotton cloth 3 times, paper 7.1 times, sugar 4.5 times, and salt 3.5 times. The targets for such major industrial products as coal, timber and salt which were originally set for 1962 in the Second Five-Year Plan, were fulfilled in 1958, four years ahead of schedule. The targets for many other major products set for 1962 in the Second Five-Year Plan will be nearly fulfilled, fulfilled, or overfulfilled by the end of 1959. The target for gross industrial output value can also be overfulfilled.

The state has paid great attention to developing industry in the areas inhabited by the national minorities with good results. The gross industrial output value in the national minority areas throughout the country in 1958 reached 5,350 million yuan, 84 per cent higher than in 1957 and 10 times the 1949 figure. The situation whereby no modern industry existed in the national minority areas has begun to change.

What has been achieved in New China in the past ten years has far surpassed the level attained in 100 years in old China. In half a century, from the end of the 19th century when old China first began to set up a modern metallurgical industry, to 1949, the annual output of steel reached only 158,000 tons. Even the peak annual output was only 923,000 tons. In the ten years from 1949 to 1959, New China has increased her steel output from 158,000 tons to 12 million tons.* In the more than fifty years from the end of the 19th century when the first mechanized colliery was built, to 1949, old China's annual output of coal reached only 32,430,000 tons, with a peak annual output of no more than 61,880,000 tons. In the ten years from 1949 to 1959, New China increased her coal output from 32,430,000 tons to 335 million tons.* In the 67 years from 1882 when the first power plant was built in Shanghai by foreign merchants, to 1949, the electric power generated annually in old China reached only 4,310 million kwh. The peak annual output was only 5,960 million kwh. But in one decade New China increased her output of electric power from 4,310 million kwh. to 39,000 million kwh.* In the 100 years from 1850, when foreign merchants began to set up a machine repair industry in China, to 1949, old China's annual output of machine tools reached only 1,582 units, with the peak annual output not exceeding 5,390 units. In the past ten years, New China increased her output of machine tools from 1,582 units to 60,000 units.* These figures clearly show how the socialist system has promoted the very rapid growth of China's social productive forces and what immeasurable strength an emancipated people have.

---

* Planned figure.

China's high rate of industrial growth has never been and can never be attained under the capitalist system. Comparing 1958 with 1949, China's industrial production increased 9.3 times. In the corresponding period, industrial production increased only 39 per cent in the United States and 29.5 per cent in Britain. In a few years, China covered the distance that had taken the capitalist countries several dozen years to travel. Take steel as an example. In Britain, the annual output of steel reached 1,310,000 tons as early as 1880. But it did not reach 7,970,000 tons until 1914. The United States' steel output was 1,270,000 tons in 1880. It was increased to 7,270,000 tons by 1897. China's steel output in 1952 was 1,350,000 tons. It was increased to 8,000,000 tons (not including steel produced by indigenous methods) by 1958. This means that in steel production, it took Britain 34 years and the United States 17 years to achieve what China accomplished in 6 years. Britain's coal output was 65,700,000 tons in 1854. But it did not grow to 270 million tons until 1907. The coal output of the United States already reached 64,800,000 tons by 1880. But it did not grow to 270 million tons until 1902. China's coal output increased from 66,490,000 tons in 1952 to 270 million tons in 1958. This means that what took Britain 53 years and the United States 22 years to do, China did in 6 years. Britain's coal production twice approached 300 million tons early in the 20th century. But in the last 20 years and more, it has been steadily declining or at a standstill. In 1958, Britain's output of coal was only about 220 million tons, falling below China.

The high rate of growth of China's industrial production has resulted in a big promotion in China's position in world industrial production. In steel output, China rose from 26th place in 1949 to 18th place in 1952 and 7th place in 1958. In coal production, China rose from 9th place in 1949 to 6th place in 1952 and 3rd place in 1958, surpassed only by the Soviet Union and the United States. In electric power generation, China rose from 25th place in 1949 to 22nd place in 1952 and

11th place in 1958. In the production of other products, China's place has steadily risen in the world scale.

Because a large number of newly-built and reconstructed enterprises have been put into operation in the last ten years and because the broad masses of workers and other employees have constantly raised their technical level and given full play to their creative spirit, China has turned out tens of thousands of new industrial products which had never been made in China before. The iron and steel industry has produced such important products as high-grade structural alloy steel, special steel for meters, silicon steel sheet, steel plate for shipbuilding, seamless steel tubes for boilers, 550 mm.-high large I-steel, and 50-kilogramme rails. Before liberation China could produce less than 100 kinds of steel; she produced 500 kinds of steel in 1958. The varieties of rolled steel increased from 400 in 1952 to 4,000 in 1957 and 6,000 in 1958, 15 times the 1952 figure. China's machine-building industry can now make aircraft, motor vehicles, tractors, sea-borne vessels of 5,000 deadweight tons, equipment for a blast furnace of 1,513 cubic metres in volume, 2,300 mm. medium-sized steel plate rolling machines, 50,000 kw. thermal power generating equipment, 72,500 kw. hydro-electric power generating equipment, 2,500-ton hydraulic forging presses, coal-cutting combines, many types of modern heavy machine tools, complete sets of textile, paper-making and sugar-refining equipment and other products. The chemical industry can now produce synthetic fibres, various kinds of antibiotics, dyestuffs with reactive colours, and organo-silicon resins, a high-grade insulating material. Old China had to import all these products from foreign countries.

As a result of the increase in the output and variety of industrial products, the ratio of self-sufficiency in materials and equipment has been greatly raised. By 1957, China's ratio of self-sufficiency in rolled steel had already reached 86 per cent and in machinery equipment the ratio rose more than 60 per cent. It can be expected that in the near future China's heavy industry will be able to supply all the technical equipment needed by industry, agriculture, transport, communications and other departments.

In the last ten years, as a result of the initiative and creative spirit demonstrated by the masses of the workers and other employees in industry in their work and improvements in the methods of management and organization, new production records have been made constantly and technical-economic norms have risen continuously. In 1958, the output, in 24 hours, of iron per cubic metre of available volume of large and medium-sized blast furnaces reached 1.49 tons, 2.4 times the 1949 figure. The output, in 24 hours, of steel per square metre of the hearth floor of the open-hearth furnaces reached 7.78 tons, 3.2 times the 1949 figure. The rate of recovery of the coal industry reached 82.7 per cent, 31.1 per cent higher than in 1949. The average annual utilization hours of the power generating equipment in the electric power industry was 2.4 times the 1949 figure and the consumption of standard coal (7,000 K calories per kg.) in power generation was 45.2 per cent lower. As for the textile industry, the output of cotton yarn per 1,000 spindles per hour reached 23.48 kilogrammes (various counts), 41.4 per cent higher than in 1949.

In the last ten years, the ranks of China's industrial workers and other employees have grown to an unprecedented size, particularly in relation to technical personnel. In 1958, the number of industrial engineers and technicians totalled 259,000, 4.5 times that of 1952. At the same time, the technical equipment has been increased markedly. During the period of the First Five-Year Plan, the average fixed assets for production per worker increased 49 per cent; the total capacity of power machinery used per worker increased 79 per cent; and the amount of electric power used per worker increased more than 80 per cent. Work which formerly required strenuous manual labour was in large part mechanized. In 1958, the technical equipment of the workers in large and medium-sized enterprises was further increased.

Labour productivity in industry has been rising continuously during the past decade. In industrial enterprises at county level and above, labour productivity in 1958 was 8 per cent higher than in 1957 and 64 per cent higher than in 1952. In the industrial departments under Central Government control the labour productivity, in physical terms, of the production workers rose in 1958 in comparison with 1949 as follows: the average daily output per miner increased 3.4 times; the average annual output per iron worker increased 17 times; and the average annual output per steel worker increased 8.6 times.

RAPID GROWTH OF INDUSTRIAL OUTPUT AND PRIORITY DEVELOPMENT OF THE MEANS OF PRODUCTION (I)

(million yuan)

	Gross output value of industry	Of which:	
		Output value of means of production	Output value of consumer goods
At 1952 prices			
1949	14,020	3,730	10,290
1950	19,120	5,650	13,470
1951	26,350	8,500	17,850
1952	34,330	12,220	22,110
1953	44,700	16,680	28,020
1954	51,970	19,990	31,980
1955	54,870	22,890	31,980
1956	70,360	32,040	38,320
1957	78,390	37,940	40,450
At 1957 prices			
1957	70,400	33,000	37,400
1958	117,000	67,000	50,000

RAPID GROWTH OF INDUSTRIAL OUTPUT AND PRIORITY DEVELOPMENT OF THE MEANS OF PRODUCTION (II)

(index numbers)

	Gross output value of industry	Of which:	
		Output value of means of production	Output value of consumer goods
(1949=100)			
1950	136.4	151.6	130.8
1951	188.0	228.0	173.5
1952	244.9	327.8	214.8
1953	318.8	447.5	272.2
1954	370.8	536.3	310.8
1955	391.4	614.2	310.7
1956	501.9	859.7	372.4
1957	559.2	1,020.0	393.0
1958	929.4	2,070.0	525.4
(1952=100)			
1953	130.2	136.5	126.7
1954	151.4	163.6	144.7
1955	159.9	187.3	144.7
1956	205.0	262.2	173.3
1957	228.4	310.5	183.0
1958	379.6	630.3	244.7

RAPID GROWTH OF INDUSTRIAL OUTPUT AND PRIORITY DEVELOPMENT OF THE MEANS OF PRODUCTION (III)

(index numbers; preceding year = 100)

	Gross output value of industry	Of which:	
		Output value of means of production	Output value of consumer goods
1950	136.4	151.6	130.8
1951	137.9	150.3	132.6
1952	130.3	143.8	123.8
1953	130.2	136.5	126.7
1954	116.3	119.8	114.2
1955	105.6	114.5	99.97
1956	128.2	140.0	119.8
1957	111.4	118.4	105.6
1958	166.2	203.0	133.7

RAPID GROWTH OF INDUSTRIAL OUTPUT AND PRIORITY DEVELOPMENT OF THE MEANS OF PRODUCTION (IV)

(average annual percentage increase)

	Gross output value of industry	Of which:	
		Output value of means of production	Output value of consumer goods
1950-1952	34.8	48.5	29.0
1953-1957	18.0	25.4	12.8
1950-1958	28.1	40.0	20.2

[89]

RAPID GROWTH OF INDUSTRIAL OUTPUT AND PRIORITY DEVELOPMENT OF THE MEANS OF PRODUCTION (V)

(percentage distribution)

	Output value of means of production	Output value of consumer goods
1949	26.6	73.4
1950	29.6	70.4
1951	32.2	67.8
1952	35.6	64.4
1953	37.3	62.7
1954	38.5	61.5
1955	41.7	58.3
1956	45.5	54.5
1957	48.4	51.6
1958	57.3	42.7

GROWTH OF MODERN INDUSTRY

	Gross output value of modern industry (million yuan)	Index numbers (1949=100)	Percentage of gross output value of modern industry to total gross output value of industry
At 1952 Prices			
1949	7,910	100	56.4
1950	10,890	137.5	56.9
1951	15,910	201.0	60.4
1952	22,050	278.6	64.2
1953	28,810	364.1	64.5
1954	33,980	429.5	65.4
1955	37,080	468.6	67.6
1956	50,340	636.2	71.6
1957	55,630	703.1	70.9
At 1957 prices			
1957	49,670	—	—
1958	87,270	1,240.0	74.6

PERCENTAGE OF SELECTED INDUSTRIES TO TOTAL GROSS OUTPUT VALUE OF INDUSTRY

	1949	1952	1957
Gross output value of industry[1]	100	100	100
Of which:			
Electric power industry	2.4	1.6	1.7
Fuel industry	3.8	3.8	4.1
Ferrous metals industry	1.8	5.1	8.0
Metal processing industry	6.8	10.6	16.2
Of which:			
Machine-building industry	2.7	5.2	9.5
Chemical industry	1.5	3.2	6.6
Building material industry	1.1	2.3	2.5
Timber industry	6.9	4.5	3.0
Paper-making industry	1.3	2.4	2.6
Textile industry	36.9	29.7	19.1
Food industry	23.6	22.6	20.4
Publishing, art supplies and educational appliances industries	3.0	2.1	2.1

[1]Handicrafts are not included.

FIXED ASSETS OF INDUSTRIAL ENTERPRISES
(at original purchase prices)

	Fixed assets of industrial enterprises	Of which: fixed assets used for industrial production
1. Absolute figures (million yuan)		
1949	12,800	—
1952	15,800	13,300
1957	35,200	29,300
1958	47,400	40,400
2. Index numbers		
(1949=100)		
1952	123	—
1957	275	—
1958	370	—
(1952=100)		
1957	223	220
1958	300	304
(1957=100)		
1958	135	138

DEVELOPMENT OF HANDICRAFTS

	Gross output value of handicrafts (million yuan)	Index numbers	
		1949=100	1952=100
1949	3,240	—	—
1950	5,060	156.4	—
1951	6,140	189.7	—
1952	7,310	225.9	—
1953	9,120	281.7	124.7
1954	10,460	323.1	143.1
1955	10,120	312.7	138.4
1956	11,700	361.5	160.1
1957	13,370	412.9	182.8

RAPID DEVELOPMENT OF INDUSTRY IN NATIONAL MINORITY AREAS

	Gross output value of industry (million yuan)	Index numbers	
		1949=100	1952=100
1949	540	100	—
1952	1,140	211	100
1957	2,950	544	258
1958	5,350	1,000	474

INCREASE IN THE OUTPUT OF MAJOR PRODUCTS

	Steel (thousand tons)	Pig iron (thousand tons)	Coal (thousand tons)	Electric power (million kwh.)	Crude petroleum (thousand tons)
1. Output					
1949	158	252	32,430	4,310	121
1950	606	978	42,920	4,550	200
1951	896	1,448	53,090	5,750	305
1952	1,349	1,929	66,490	7,260	436
1953	1,774	2,234	69,680	9,200	622
1954	2,225	3,114	83,660	11,000	789
1955	2,853	3,872	98,300	12,280	966
1956	4,465	4,826	110,360	16,590	1,163
1957	5,350	5,936	130,000	19,340	1,458
1958	11,080 (8,000)	13,690 (9,530)	270,000	27,530	2,264
2. Index numbers					
(1949=100)					
1952	853.8	765.5	205.0	168.4	360.3
1957	3,390.0	2,360.0	400.9	448.8	1,210.0
1958	7,010.0 (5,060.0)	5,430.0 (3,780.0)	832.6	639.1	1,870.0
(1952=100)					
1957	396.6	307.7	195.5	266.3	334.7
1958	821.3 (593.0)	709.7 (494.0)	406.1	379.2	520.0
(1957=100)					
1958	207.1 (149.5)	230.6 (160.5)	207.7	142.4	155.4

Note: The figures for the output of steel and pig iron in 1958 include steel and iron produced by indigenous methods. The figures within parentheses do not include steel and iron produced by indigenous methods

[95]

	Cement (thousand tons)	Timber (thousand cubic metres)	Sulphuric acid (thousand tons)	Soda-ash (thousand tons)	Caustic soda (thousand tons)
1. Output					
1949	660	5,670	40	88	15
1950	1,410	6,640	49	160	23
1951	2,490	7,640	149	185	48
1952	2,860	11,200	190	192	79
1953	3,880	17,530	260	223	88
1954	4,600	22,210	344	309	115
1955	4,500	20,930	375	405	137
1956	6,390	20,840	517	476	156
1957	6,860	27,870	632	506	198
1958	9,300	35,000	740	640	270
2. Index numbers					
(1949 = 100)					
1952	433.3	197.5	475.0	218.2	526.7
1957	1,040.0	491.5	1,580.0	575.0	1,320.0
1958	1,410.0	617.3	1,850.0	727.3	1,800.0
(1952 = 100)					
1957	239.9	248.8	332.6	263.5	250.6
1958	325.2	312.5	389.5	333.3	341.8
(1957 = 100)					
1958	135.6	125.6	117.1	126.5	136.4

INCREASE IN THE OUTPUT OF MAJOR PRODUCTS (cont'd)

	Chemical fertilizers (thousand tons)	Penicillin (kilogrammes)	Metal-cutting machine tools (number)	Power machinery (thousand h.p.)	Electric motors (thousand kw.)
1.Output					
1949	27	—	1,582	10	61
1950	70	—	3,312	11	199
1951	129	—	5,853	26	225
1952	181	46	13,734	35	639
1953	226	593	20,502	144	918
1954	298	2,189	15,901	172	957
1955	332	7,829	13,708	247	607
1956	523	14,037	25,928	657	1,069
1957	631	18,266	28,000	690	1,455
1958	811	72,607	50,000	2,000	6,052
2.Index numbers					
(1949 = 100)					
1952	670.4	—	868.1	350.0	1,050.0
1957	2,340.0	—	1,770.0	6,900.0	2,390.0
1958	3,000.0	—	3,160.0	20,000.0	9,920.0
(1952 = 100)					
1957	348.6	39,710.0	203.9	1,970.0	227.7
1958	448.1	157,800.0	.364.1	5,710.0	947.1
(1957 = 100)					
1958	128.5	397.5	178.6	289.9	415.9

Note: Chemical fertilizers do not include ammonium nitrate. Metal-cutting machine tools do not include simple indigenous machine tools.

[97]

INCREASE IN THE OUTPUT OF MAJOR PRODUCTS (cont'd)

	Power generating equipment (thousand kw.)	Locomotives (number)	Motor vehicles (number)	Merchant vessels (thousand dwt. tons)	Tractors (number)	Combine harvesters (number)
1. Output						
1952	—	20	—	16	—	—
1953	—	10	—	35	—	—
1954	—	52	—	62	—	—
1955	—	98	—	120	—	3
1956	—	184	1,654	104	—	22
1957	198	167	7,500	54	—	124
1958	800	350	16,000	90	957	545
2. Index numbers						
(1952=100)						
1957	—	835.0	—	337.5	—	—
1958	—	1,750.0	—	562.5	—	—
(1957=100)						
1958	404.0	209.6	213.3	166.7	—	439.5

INCREASE IN THE OUTPUT OF MAJOR PRODUCTS (cont'd)

	Cotton yarn (thousand bales)	Cotton cloth (million metres)	Paper (thousand tons)	Rubber foot-wear (thousand pairs)	Bicycles (thousand units)
1.Output					
1949	1,800	1,890	228	28,900	14
1950	2,410	2,520	380	45,670	21
1951	2,680	3,060	492	65,060	44
1952	3,620	3,830	539	61,690	80
1953	4,100	4,690	667	76,360	165
1954	4,600	5,230	842	85,840	298
1955	3,970	4,360	839	97,450	335
1956	5,250	5,770	998	103,480	640
1957	4,650	·5,050	1,221	128,850	806
1958	6,100	5,700	1,630	182,360	1,174
2.Index numbers					
(1949=100)					
1952	200.7	202.7	236.3	213.5	568.2
1957	258.1	267.4	535.7	445.9	5,720.0
1958	338.3	301.8	714.9	631.1	8,340.0
(1952=100)					
1957	128.6	131.9	226.7	208.9	1,010.0
1958	168.6	148.9	302.5	295.6	1,470.0
(1957=100)					
1958	131.1	112.9	133.5	141.5	145.7

Note: Paper includes cardboard.

	Cigarettes (thousand crates)[1]	Edible vegetable oil (thousand tons)	Sugar (thousand tons)	Salt (thousand tons)	Aquatic products (thousand tons)
1. Output					
1949	1,600	444	199	2,985	448
1950	1,848	607	242	2,464	912
1951	2,002	731	300	4,346	1,332
1952	2,650	983	451	4,945	1,666
1953	3,552	1,009	638	3,569.	1,900
1954	3,728	1,066	693	4,886	2,293
1955	3,567	1,165	717	7,535	2,518
1956	3,907	1,076	807	4,940	2,648
1957	4,456	1,100	864	8,277	3,120
1958	4,750	1,250	900	10,400	4,060
2. Index numbers					
(1949=100)					
1952	165.6	221.5	226.5	165.7	372.0
1957	278.5	247.9	434.1	277.3	695.7
1958	296.9	281.7	451.9	348.4	906.4
(1952=100)					
1957	168.2	111.9	191.6	167.4	187.0
1958	179.3	127.2	199.5	210.3	243.7
(1957=100)					
1958	106.6	113.6	104.1	125.7	130.3

[1] One crate contains 50,000 cigarettes.

AVERAGE ANNUAL RATE OF INCREASE IN OUTPUT OF MAJOR PRODUCTS

(percentage)

	1950–1952	1953–1957	1950–1958
Steel	104.2	31.7	60.4 (54.7)
Pig iron	97.1	25.2	55.9 (49.7)
Coal	27.0	14.4	26.6
Electric power	18.9	21.6	22.9
Crude petroleum	53.3	27.3	38.5
Cement	63.1	19.1	34.2
Timber	25.5	20.0	22.4
Sulphuric acid	68.1	27.1	38.3
Soda-ash	29.7	21.4	24.7
Caustic soda	74.0	20.1	37.9
Chemical fertilizers (not including ammonium nitrate)	88.6	28.4	46.0
Penicillin	—	231.0	—
Metal-cutting machine tools	105.0	15.3	46.7

Note: The average annual percentage increases for steel and iron in the 1950-1958 column include steel and iron produced by indigenous method, while the percentage increases in parentheses do not.

AVERAGE ANNUAL RATE OF INCREASE IN OUTPUT OF MAJOR PRODUCTS (cont'd)

(percentage)

	1950–1952	1953–1957	1950–1958
Power machinery	51.8	81.5	80.2
Electric motors	119.0	17.9	66.6
Locomotives	—	52.9	—
Merchant vessels	—	27.5	—
Cotton yarn	26.1	5.2	14.5
Cotton cloth	26.6	5.7	13.1
Paper	33.2	17.8	24.4
Rubber foot-wear	28.8	15.9	22.7
Bicycles	78.4	58.8	63.5
Cigarettes	18.3	11.0	12.8
Edible vegetable oil	30.4	2.3	12.2
Sugar	31.3	13.9	18.3
Salt	18.3	10.9	14.9
Aquatic products	54.9	13.3	27.8

OUTPUT OF MAJOR INDUSTRIAL PRODUCTS COMPARED WITH PEAK PRE-LIBERATION OUTPUT

	Unit	Peak pre-liberation output	Index numbers (peak pre-liberation year=100)			
			1949	1952	1957	1958
Steel	thousand tons	923	17.1	146.2	579.6	1,200.0 (866.7)
Pig iron	do	1,801	14.0	107.1	329.6	760.1 (529.2)
Coal	do	61,880	52.4	107.4	210.1	436.3
Electric power	million kwh.	5,960	72.3	121.9	324.4	462.3
Crude petroleum	thousand tons	321	37.7	135.7	454.2	705.7
Cement	do	2,290	28.8	124.9	299.6	406.1
Sulphuric acid	do	180	22.2	105.6	351.1	411.1
Soda-ash	do	103	85.4	186.4	491.3	621.4
Caustic soda	do	12	125.0	658.3	1,650.0	2,250.0
Chemical fertilizers	do	227	11.9	79.7	278.0	357.3
Metal-cutting machine tools	number	5,390	29.4	254.8	519.5	927.6
Cotton yarn	thousand bales	2,450	73.7	147.8	190.1	249.3
Cotton cloth	million metres	2,790	67.8	137.4	181.2	204.5
Cigarettes	thousand crates[1]	2,363	67.7	112.1	188.6	201.0
Sugar	thousand tons	414	48.1	109.0	208.8	217.4
Salt	do	3,918	76.2	126.2	211.2	265.4

[1]One crate contains 50,000 cigarettes.

PRINCIPAL NEW PRODUCTS SUCCESSFULLY TRIAL-MANUFACTURED

Year	Products
1953	43-kg. heavy rail, 6,000 kw. water-turbine generator, 44 kv.-20,000 KVA transformer, 500 mm.-swing heavy duty lathe, double column planer with a planing length of 4 metres, radial drilling machine with a drilling diameter of 50 mm., 1,000 metre-drilling machine, rotary cone crusher with a diameter of 2,100 mm., 2,700 x 2,100 ball mill, large X-ray apparatus, penicillin in oil, aniline, glacial acetic acid and wall board.
1954	Heat-resistant stainless steel, 6,000 kw. steam-turbine generator, 154 kv.-20,000 KVA transformer, special purpose multi-cutter semi-automatic lathe, horizontal boring, drilling and milling machine with a main spindle of 85 mm. in diameter, hydraulic precision grinder, coal-cutting combine, coal loading machine, 300 h.p. hoisting machine for mines, ladle for molten iron with a capacity of 100 tons, pneumatic ore loading machine which can load 20 cubic metres of ore per hour, 0.3 cubic-metre electric mud gun, spiral grading machine 1,200 mm. in diameter, freighter of 2,650 tons displacement, training plane, 24-row sower, centralite, phenacetin, rubber tire with cross sectional width of 12 in. and an internal diameter of 22 in. and, toughened glass.
1955	Steel plate for shipbuilding, special-shape rolled steel for motor vehicles, 50-kg. heavy rails, seamless alloy steel tube, silicon steel sheet, water-tube boiler which can evaporate 40 tons of steam per hour, 6,000 kw. steam turbine, 10,000 kw. water-turbine generator and water turbine, 120 kv.-31,500 KVA transformer, universal slotting machine, single.spindle automatic lathe and 58 other types of machine tools, ore sintering furnace with a capacity of 90 tons per hour, mining axial-flow ventilator 2.4 metres in diameter, coke loader, 48-row sower, 5-share plough, combine harvester, syntomycin and sodium nitrate.

PRINCIPAL NEW PRODUCTS SUCCESSFULLY TRIAL-MANUFACTURED (cont'd)

Year	Products
1956	High-temperature resistant alloy steel, 12,000 kw. steam-turbine generator and steam turbine, 15,000 kw. water-turbine generator and water turbine, 600 h.p. Diesel engine, double column planer with a planing width of 2 metres, 120 kw. short-wave broadcasting transmitter, lorry, 1-5-1 freight locomotive, jet plane, organic glass, P V C (poly-vinyl chloride), aureomycin, acetone, laminated glass and wrist watch.
1957	Steel plate for motor vehicles, water-tube boiler which can evaporate 130 tons of steam per hour, 220 kv.-20,000 KVA single-phase transformer, 140-ton overhead hoisting crane, 3 cubic-metre electric shovel, 1,200-metre petroleum drilling machine, equipment for blast furnace of 1,000 cubic metres in volume, An-II planes for various purposes, 70 types of machine tools, methyl alcohol, variamine B, penicillin, camera, synthetic wool and synthetic leather.
1958	Various kinds of low-alloy high-strength structural steel, clad stainless sheet steel, 550 mm.-high large I-steel, 25,000 kw. thermal power generating equipment, 110 kv.-60,000 KVA 3-phase transformer, 220 kv.-40,000 KVA single-phase transformer, blast furnace of 1,513 cubic metres in volume, 2,300 mm. medium-sized plate rolling machine, 2,500-ton hydraulic forging press, ocean-going ship of 5,000 tons deadweight, dye-stuffs with reactive colours, organo-silicon resins—a high grade insulating material, tubeless tire, chloroprene rubber, high-grade cement and synthetic detergent.

CHINA'S PLACE IN WORLD OUTPUT OF STEEL, PIG IRON, COAL AND ELECTRIC POWER

	Steel	Pig iron	Coal	Electric power
1936	18th	12th	7th	14th
1949	26th	23rd	9th	25th
1952	18th	11th	6th	22nd
1957	9th	7th	5th	13th
1958	7th	6th	3rd	11th

CHINA FAR SURPASSES THE CAPITALIST COUNTRIES IN THE RATE OF GROWTH OF INDUSTRIAL OUTPUT

(percentage)

	1950–1952 average annual rate of growth	1953–1957 average annual rate of growth	Percentage increase in 1958 over 1957	1950–1958 average annual rate of growth
Industrial output:				
China	34.8	18.0	66.2	28.1
Britain	2.2	4.1	0.9	2.9
United States	8.5	2.8	−6.5	3.7
Steel:				
China	104.2	31.7	49.5	54.7
Britain	1.8	5.7	−9.8	2.6
United States	6.1	3.9	−24.5	1.0
Pig iron:				
China	97.1	25.2	60.5	49.7
Britain	4.2	5.9	−9.2	3.5
United States	4.9	5.0	−27.1	0.8
Coal:				
China	27.0	14.4	107.7	26.6
Britain	1.7	decline	−3.5	0.03
United States	1.8	0.4	−17.6	decline
Electricity:				
China	18.9	21.6	42.4	22.9
Britain	8.2	7.8	7.4	7.9
United States	10.3	9.1	1.2	8.6

[107]

PRINCIPAL NORMS IN VARIOUS INDUSTRIAL DEPARTMENTS

	Unit	1949	1952	1957	1958
Iron and steel industry					
Coefficient of utilization of blast furnaces[1]	ton/cu. metre in 24 hrs.	0.62	1.02	1.32	1.49
Coefficient of utilization of open-hearth furnaces	ton/sq. metre in 24 hrs.	2.42	4.78	7.21	7.78
Coal industry					
Recovery rate[2]	%	63.1	76	81.9	82.7
Electric power industry					
Utilizing hours of power generating equipment	hours	2,330	3,800	4,794	5,518
Consumption of standard coal	kg./kwh.	1.020	0.727	0.604	0.559
Of which: consumption of standard coal by public utility power plants	kg./kwh.	0.961	0.685	0.573	0.537
Building material industry					
Output of cement kilns per square metre per hour	kg.			22.69	23.34

[1]For large and medium-sized blast furnaces,
[2]For large and medium-sized coal mines.

PRINCIPAL NORMS IN VARIOUS INDUSTRIAL DEPARTMENTS (cont'd)

	Unit	1949	1952	1957	1958
Machine-building industry					
Rate of utilization of metal-cutting machine tools[1]	%		58.8	64.8	82.9
Textile industry					
Output of cotton yarn per thousand spindles per hour	kg.	16.60	19.64	20.67	23.48
Output of cotton cloth per loom per hour	metres	3.516	3.988	4.075	4.160
Consumption of cotton per bale of yarn	kg.	205.85	198.97	193.56	192.85

[1]1953 figure.

ADVANCE IN OVER-ALL LABOUR PRODUCTIVITY IN INDUSTRY

	1957 (1952=100)	1958 (1957=100)	1958 (1952=100)
Labour productivity	152	108	164

Note: Data cover workers and other employees in industrial enterprises at county level and above.

GROWTH OF LABOUR PRODUCTIVITY IN PHYSICAL TERMS

	1957 (1952=100)	1958 (1949=100)
Average daily output per coal miner	145.8	341.7
Average annual output per iron worker	238.5	1,698.5
Average annual output per steel worker	192.9	857.7
Average annual output per cement worker	174.3	—
Average annual output of cotton yarn per spinner	108.0	—

Note: Data cover enterprises directly under the industrial departments of the Central Government.

INCREASE IN TECHNICAL EQUIPMENT PER WORKER IN INDUSTRY IN 1957

(1952 = 100)

Average amount of fixed assets used per worker 149.1
Total capacity of power machinery used per worker 179.2
Total amount of electricity used per worker 180.4

[110]

COST REDUCTION OF INDUSTRIAL PRODUCTS

(percentage)

	Percentage reduction in 1957 over 1952	Average annual rate of reduction 1953-1957
Total cost of comparable products of industrial departments under central authorities	29	6.5
Of which: unit cost of principal products		
Electric power (one thousand kwh.)	24.5	5.5
No. 56 motor petrol (one ton)	1.3	0.3
Pig iron (one ton)	2.6	0.5
Medium-sized rolled steel (one ton)	28.1	6.4
Welded steel tube (one ton)	47.5	12.1
Oil of vitriol (98%) (one ton)	18.7	4.1
Caustic soda (95-98%) (one ton)	31.6	7.3
Ammonium nitrate (above 90%) (one ton)	42.5	10.5
32-count cotton yarn (one bale)	4.2	0.9
23 × 21 cotton cloth (one bolt)	4.6	0.9
No. 1 newsprint (one ton)	33.0	7.7

V. TREMENDOUS GROWTH OF SOCIALIST AGRICULTURE

As a result of the basic changes in the relations of production in agriculture which have taken place during the past ten years, and the heightened enthusiasm for labour and creativeness on the part of the broad masses of the peasants, China has made tremendous progress in agricultural production. The big leap in agriculture in 1958 was an achievement unmatched in Chinese history.

The reform of feudal ownership of the land was completed in the short time of three years after the founding of the People's Republic of China. This in turn released the productive forces in the countryside and hastened the recovery and development of agricultural production. By 1952 the output of grain, cotton and several other principal crops caught up with and surpassed the pre-liberation peak levels. During the First Five-Year Plan, along with the successful completion of agricultural co-operation, fresh progress was achieved in agricultural production. In 1957, grain output totalled 370,000 million catties, an increase of 20 per cent over 1952. The cotton output in 1957 reached 32.8 million *tan*, an increase of 26 per cent over 1952. Remarkable increases were also achieved in the output of other crops in comparison with 1952.

In 1958 the Chinese peasants created a new form of social organization — the people's commune — and agricultural output rose to new heights. The gross output value of agriculture in 1958 reached 67,100 million yuan, exceeding that of 1957 by 25 per cent, or 2.3 times the 1949 gross output value, an average annual rate of increase of 9.8 per cent. The total output of grain was 500,000 million catties, an increase of 35 per cent over 1957, or 2.3 times the 1949 figure, an average annual rate of increase of 9.8 per cent. The total output of cotton reached 42 million *tan*, representing an increase of 28 per cent over 1957, or 4.7 times the 1949 output of cotton, an average annual rate of increase of 18.8 per cent. In comparison with 1949 the increases in output of other principal crops in 1958 were as follows: soya beans, 110 per cent; groundnuts, 120 per cent; rapeseed, 50 per cent; sugar beet, 1,420 per cent; sugar-cane, 410 per cent; cured tobacco, 780 per cent; jute and ambary hemp, 740 per cent.

Such a rapid rate of increase in agricultural production was not only unknown in old China, but was never attained and cannot be attained in capitalist countries. In comparison with 1949, the grain output in China in 1958 increased 131.3 per cent. In the corresponding period the grain output in the United States increased only 25.2 per cent, while in Britain the grain output did not increase, but declined 6.5 per cent. In comparison with 1949, the cotton output in China in 1958 shot up 372.4 per cent, while cotton output in the United States declined 28.1 per cent in the same period.

In the past decade China also made tremendous progress in livestock-breeding. In 1958 the total number of draught animals (i.e. oxen, horses, mules, donkeys, etc.) reached more than 85 million head, an increase of 42 per cent over 1949. At that time there were 160 million pigs, and 108,860,000 goats and sheep, representing increases of 180 per cent and 160 per cent respectively over 1949.

Great achievements have also been made in afforestation. In response to the Government's call to make China green, the broad masses of people have carried out a nation-wide movement to plant trees. During the nine years between 1950 and 1958 the Chinese people afforested close to 500 million *mou* of land. In 1958 alone they planted 260 million *mou* of trees, more than the aggregate area afforested in the previous eight years.

In the past decade the government authorities and the peasants have undertaken large-scale water conservancy and irrigation works. These projects have not only greatly increased the flood-control facilities and lessened the threat of flood disasters, but also played a significant role in the fight against drought and extended the irrigated areas, which, in turn, ensured a rapid growth of agricultural production. By the end of 1958 the total irrigated area of China reached 1,000 million *mou,* or 60 per cent of the total area of arable land. During the nine years between 1950 and 1958 the newly irrigated area amounted to 780 million *mou,* three times more than the total area brought under irrigation in the thousands of years before liberation. In 1958 alone the irrigated land throughout the country increased by 480 million *mou,* more than the total area irrigated during the previous eight years.

The rapid growth of agricultural production is inseparable from the tremendous assistance given the peasants by the Government. During the past ten years the Government made heavy investments in water conservancy works, agriculture and forestry, supplied large quantities of farm tools and fertilizers, loaned large sums of money for agricultural purposes and set up a number of rural enterprises and public services. During the nine years between 1950 and 1958 the Government granted close to 12,600 million yuan in farm loans. By the end of 1957 the state had founded 390 agricultural machine and tractor stations with 12,176 tractors in terms of 15 h.p. units, over 13,600 agricultural technical stations, more than 800 breeding stations, over 2,900 veterinary stations, and over 150 centres for promoting improved farm implements. During the big leap of 1958 there was a tremendous increase in the number of agricultural technical stations and other public services.

The same period also witnessed a tremendous improvement in agricultural productive know-how. The valuable experiences accumulated by peasants over the years in increasing per *mou* yields were summed up by Chairman Mao Tse-tung and became a guide of practical measures to increase production. This is known as the "Eight-Point Charter of Agriculture" which covers soil improvement, increased application of fertilizer, water conservancy and irrigation, seed selection, rational close planting, plant protection, field management and tools reform.

During the past decade remarkable achievements have been made in agricultural production, especially during the big leap forward of 1958 when great efforts were made to implement thoroughly the "Eight-Point Charter of Agriculture." In the case of soil improvement, a large amount of work was done on deep ploughing, soil amelioration and levelling the fields. During the autumn and winter of 1957 and the spring of 1959, 800 million *mou* of land, nearly half of the total land under cultivation, was deep-ploughed.

In the case of fertilizer, the Government organized the peasants to tap bigger resources of fertilizer by accumulating compost and various other kinds of manure. At the same time, energetic efforts were made to develop the production of chemical fertilizers to meet the peasants' increasing needs. During the seven years between 1952 and 1958 the state supplied the peasants with 9,230,000 tons of chemical fertilizers.

In the field of water conservancy, fundamental control of some of the rivers which caused recurrent floods in the past has been accomplished. In addition, large-scale water conservancy and irrigation works have been undertaken in rural areas. Thanks to these efforts, great strides have been made in fighting floods and drought. Seed selection has also received attention. In 1952 improved varieties of rice and wheat seeds were sown only to over 41 million *mou*, a little more than 5 per cent of the total area devoted to rice and wheat crops. Again in 1952, improved cotton seeds were sown to 42 million *mou*, or half the total area devoted to cotton crops that year. In 1953, improved seeds were used practically everywhere for such major crops as rice, wheat and cotton. Close planting in varying degrees was practised extensively throughout the country in 1958 and much valuable experience was gained in experiments with rational close planting. Plant protection, prevention and elimination of plant diseases and insect pests, and field management received close attention and consequently played a decisive role in ensuring increased production. Tools reform has also made considerable progress. The broad masses of peasants have shown creativeness in reforming many of the existing farm tools. At the same time they have invented and popularized many types of new farm tools. The movement launched in 1958 to replace shoulder-poles with vehicles and popularize ball-bearings was warmly welcomed by the peasants. The adoption and promotion of the foregoing measures to increase agricultural production effectively boosted the development of agriculture.

China's meteorological service has shown marked development in the past ten years. The extreme backwardness of meteorological work which was true of old China has undergone a fundamental change. In 1958 there were over 2,700 meteorological observatories and stations and weather forecasting stations, or 27 times the number existing in 1949. A network of meteorological observatories and stations and weather forecasting stations is, in the main, completed in China. The rapid growth of the meteorological service has not only played a significant role in preventing natural calamities, helping plan farm work and ensuring increased agricultural yields, but has also had a considerable influence on the smooth progress of industrial production, capital construction, transport and communications.

As a result of the rapid growth of agricultural production, especially the big leap in 1958, the National Programme for Agricultural Development which was originally planned for realization in 1967, will be carried out far ahead of schedule. By 1958 many counties and municipalities throughout the country reached the production targets laid down for them in the 12-year National Programme for Agricultural Development i.e. that the per *mou* yield of grain in the three regions of the country should reach the targets of 400, 500 and 800 catties per *mou* respectively, and in the case of cotton, 60, 80 and 100 catties per *mou* respectively.

GROWTH OF GROSS OUTPUT VALUE OF AGRICULTURE

	Absolute figures (million yuan)	Index numbers		
		1949=100	1952=100	Preceding year=100
At 1952 prices				
1949	32,590	100		
1950	38,360	117.7		117.7
1951	41,970	128.8		109.4
1952	48,390	148.5	100	115.3
1953	49,910	153.1	103.1	103.1
1954	51,570	158.2	106.6	103.3
1955	55,540	170.4	114.8	107.7
1956	58,290	178.8	120.4	104.9
1957	60,350	185.1	124.7	103.5
At 1957 prices				
1957	53,700	—	—	—
1958	67,100	231.4	155.9	125.0

OUTPUT OF GRAIN CROPS AND COTTON (I)

(absolute figures)

	Grain crops (million catties)	Of which:				Cotton (thousand *tan*)
		Rice (unhusked)	Wheat	Coarse grains	Potatoes	
Pre-liberation peak year	277,400	114,700	46,600	103,400	12,700	16,980
1949	216,200	97,300	27,600	71,600	19,700	8,890
1950	249,400	110,200	29,000	85,400	24,800	13,850
1951	270,100	121,100	34,500	86,500	28,000	20,610
1952	308,800	136,900	36,200	103,000	32,700	26,070
1953	313,800	142,500	36,600	101,400	33,300	23,490
1954	320,900	141,700	46,700	98,500	34,000	21,300
1955	349,600	156,000	45,900	109,900	37,800	30,370
1956	365,000	164,900	49,600	106,800	43,700	28,900
1957	370,000	173,600	47,300	105,300	43,800	32,800
1958	500,000	227,400	57,900	123,900	90,800	42,000

Note: In calculating the output of grain crops, potatoes are converted into grain-equivalent at the ratio of four catties to one. Cotton: ginned cotton.

OUTPUT OF GRAIN CROPS AND COTTON (II)

(index numbers)

	Grain crops	Of which:				Cotton
		Rice (unhusked)	Wheat	Coarse grains	Potatoes	
(Pre-liberation peak year=100)						
1949	77.9	84.8	59.3	69.2	155.5	52.4
1952	111.3	119.3	77.8	99.6	257.9	153.6
1957	133.4	151.3	101.5	101.8	346.2	193.2
1958	180.2	198.3	124.2	119.8	715.0	247.3
(1949=100)						
1952	142.8	140.7	131.2	143.9	165.9	293.4
1957	171.1	178.4	171.2	147.1	222.7	369.0
1958	231.3	233.7	209.8	173.0	460.9	472.4
(1952=100)						
1957	119.8	126.8	130.4	102.2	134.3	125.8
1958	161.9	166.1	159.9	120.3	277.7	161.1
(1957=100)						
1958	135.1	131.0	122.4	117.7	207.3	128.0
Average annual rate of increase(%)						
1950–1952	12.6	12.1	9.5	12.9	18.4	43.2
1953–1957	3.7	4.9	5.5	0.4	6.1	4.7
1950–1958	9.8	9.9	8.6	6.3	18.5	18.8

PER *MOU* YIELD OF GRAIN CROPS AND COTTON

(catties)

	Grain crops	Of which:				Cotton
		Rice (unhusked)	Wheat	Coarse grains	Potatoes	
1949	142	252	86	101	187	22
1950	159	281	85	118	215	24
1951	168	300	100	118	225	25
1952	183	321	98	136	251	31
1953	183	336	95	132	246	30
1954	184	329	115	129	231	26
1955	197	357	115	140	251	35
1956	196	330	121	135	265	31
1957	204	359	114	139	278	38
1958	275	463	145	181	372	49

Note: The per *mou* yield is calculated on the basis of the sown areas. Potatoes are converted into grain-equivalent at the ratio of four catties to one.

COMPARATIVE STATISTICS ON GRAIN OUTPUT BETWEEN CHINA AND MAJOR CAPITALIST COUNTRIES

	China	U.S.A.	Britain	West Germany	France	Japan
Output (million catties)						
1949	216,200	303,500	21,400	31,100	33,300	35,600
1952	308,800	300,000	21,100	35,000	35,900	39,200
1957	370,000	323,900	20,300	40,000	47,000	42,200
1958	500,000	379,900	20,000	37,300	44,300	43,300
1958 (1949=100)	231.3	125.2	93.5	120.0	133.0	121.6
Average annual rate of increase from 1950 to 1958 (%)	9.8	2.5	decline	2.0	3.2	2.2

COMPARATIVE STATISTICS ON COTTON OUTPUT BETWEEN CHINA AND THE UNITED STATES

	China	U.S.A.
Output (thousand *tan*)		
1949	8,890	70,160
1952	26,070	65,640
1957	32,800	47,740
1958	42,000	50,420
1958 (1949=100)	472.4	71.9
Average annual rate of increase from 1950 to 1958 (%)	18.8	decline

OUTPUT OF SOYA BEANS AND PRINCIPAL INDUSTRIAL CROPS

	Soya beans (million catties)	Groundnuts (thousand *tan*)	Rapeseed (thousand *tan*)	Sugar-beet (thousand *tan*)	Sugar-cane (thousand *tan*)	Cured tobacco (thousand *tan*)
1. Absolute figures						
1949	10,200	25,360	14,680	3,810	52,840	860
1952	19,000	46,320	18,640	9,570	142,320	4,430
1957	20,100	51,420	17,750	30,020	207,850	5,120
1958	21,000	56,000	22,000	58,000	270,500	7,600
2. Index numbers						
(1949=100)						
1952	187.2	182.6	127.0	251.2	269.3	516.8
1957	197.5	202.7	120.9	787.9	393.3	597.1
1958	205.9	220.8	149.9	1,520.0	511.9	883.7
(1952=100)						
1957	105.5	111.0	95.2	313.7	146.0	115.5
1958	110.5	120.9	118.0	606.1	190.1	171.6
(1957=100)						
1958	104.5	108.9	123.9	193.2	130.1	148.4

OUTPUT OF TEA AND COCOONS (I)

(thousand *tan*)

	Tea	Cocoons of cultivated silkworms	Tussah cocoons
1949	820	620	240
1950	1,300	670	500
1951	1,570	940	530
1952	1,650	1,240	1,220
1953	1,690	1,190	250
1954	1,840	1,300	510
1955	2,160	1,340	1,280
1956	2,410	1,450	1,240
1957	2,230	1,360	890
1958	2,800	1,690	1,140

OUTPUT OF TEA AND COCOONS (II)

(index numbers)

	Tea	Cocoons of cultivated silkworms	Tussah cocoons
(1949=100)			
1952	200.7	201.3	513.5
1957	271.8	219.5	373.7
1958	341.5	272.6	475.0
(1952=100)			
1957	135.5	109.0	72.8
1958	169.7	136.3	93.4
(1957=100)			
1958	125.6	124.3	128.1

[126]

OUTPUT OF FRUIT (I)

(thousand *tan*)

	Total output	Of which:				
		Oranges	Apples	Pears	Bananas	Grapes
1952	48,860	4,130	2,360	7,870	2,200	970
1953	59,380	5,100	2,780	10,610	2,310	1,330
1954	59,550	6,580	3,470	4,820	2,890	1,520
1955	51,000	5,690	4,050	8,190	1,930	1,290
1956	62,100	6,320	4,410	10,510	1,970	1,600
1957	64,950	6,440	4,430	10,070	1,460	1,710
1958	78,000	8,240	5,950	15,930	3,170	2,230

OUTPUT OF FRUIT (II)

(index numbers)

	Total output	Of which:				
		Oranges	Apples	Pears	Bananas	Grapes
(1952=100)						
1957	132.9	155.8	187.6	127.9	66.6	176.5
1958	159.6	199.5	252.1	202.4	144.1	229.9
(1957=100)						
1958	120.1	128.0	134.3	158.2	217.1	130.4

[127]

CULTIVATED AREA, SOWN AREA AND RATIO OF MULTIPLE CROP AREA

	Cultivated area (thousand *mou*)	Sown area (thousand *mou*)	Ratio of multiple crop area
1949	1,468,220	...	...
1950	1,505,340	...	...
1951	1,555,070	...	...
1952	1,618,780	2,118,840	130.9
1953	1,627,930	2,160,530	132.7
1954	1,640,320	2,218,880	135.3
1955	1,652,350	2,266,220	137.2
1956	1,677,370	2,387,590	142.3
1957	1,677,450	2,358,660	140.6
1958	1,616,800	2,344,020	145.0

Note: Ratio of multiple crop area is the percentage of sown area to the cultivated area. An area may be sown more than once in a year, and each sowing is counted separately, therefore the sown area can be much larger than the cultivated area.

AREA SOWN TO GRAIN CROPS AND COTTON

(thousand *mou*)

	Grain Crops					Cotton
	Total	Rice	Wheat	Coarse grains	Potatoes	
1949	1,524,600	385,630	322,730	711,080	105,160	41,550
1950	1,572,050	392,240	342,000	722,370	115,440	56,790
1951	1,604,520	404,000	345,820	730,410	124,290	82,270
1952	1,684,490	425,730	371,700	756,740	130,320	83,640
1953	1,714,120	424,820	384,540	769,520	135,240	77,700
1954	1,745,120	430,830	404,510	763,060	146,720	81,930
1955	1,775,960	437,600	401,080	786,470	150,810	86,590
1956	1,864,390	499,680	409,080	790,760	164,870	93,830
1957	1,813,270	483,620	413,120	759,110	157,420	86,630
1958	1,819,490	491,170	399,350	684,780	244,190	85,840

EXPANSION OF IRRIGATION AND CONSERVATION OF WATER AND SOIL

	Existing irrigated area (million *mou*)	Increase in irrigated area (thousand *mou*)	Area of transformed water-logged, low-lying land (thousand *mou*)	Area under preliminary water and soil conservation (sq. km.)
1949	240	—	—	—
1950	250	12,040	—	—
1951	280	27,960	—	—
1952	320	40,180	—	—
1953	330	18,020		
1954	350	16,020	58,090	78,310
1955	370	22,260		
1956	480	118,700	84,640	73,650
1957	520	43,090	51,730	51,543
1958	1,000	480,430	206,830	318,720

PERCENTAGE OF AREA SOWN TO IMPROVED SEEDS
OF STAPLE CROPS

(total area sown to a crop = 100)

	Grain Crops	Of which:				Cotton	Oil-bearing crops
		Rice	Wheat	Coarse grains	Potatoes		
1952	4.7	5.4	5.1	5.0	0.4	50.2	1.9
1953	7.4	7.9	7.4	8.0	2.2	61.4	2.4
1954	14.9	12.0	23.5	12.9	9.9	67.7	2.9
1955	20.6	19.0	32.7	16.5	13.8	70.5	4.0
1956	36.4	41.3	58.7	21.4	38.3	89.5	31.5
1957	55.2	62.9	68.7	42.5	56.5	93.9	47.7
1958	77.5	81.9	86.1	67.9	81.5	97.0	61.6

LIVESTOCK

	Big draught animals	Sheep and goats	Pigs
1. Absolute figures (thousand head)			
Pre-liberation peak year	71,510	62,520	78,530
1949	60,020	42,350	57,750
1952	76,460	61,780	89,770
1957	83,820	98,580	145,900
1958	85,060	108,860	160,000
2. Index numbers			
(Pre-liberation peak year=100)			
1949	83.6	67.7	73.5
1952	106.5	98.8	114.3
1958	118.4	174.1	203.7
(1949=100)			
1952	127.4	145.9	155.4
1958	141.7	257.0	277.1
(1952=100)			
1957	109.6	159.6	162.5
(1957=100)			
1958	101.5	110.4	109.7

AFFORESTED AREA

(thousand *mou*)

	Afforested area			Area devoted to seedlings	Area devoted to saplings
	Total	Of which:			
		Shelter belts	Timber		
Total	**497,860**	**115,780**	**188,190**	**7,720**	**183,640**
1950	1,900	1,010	210	30	—
1951	6,760	3,790	1,150	70	—
1952	16,280	8,540	3,310	180	1,230
1953	16,690	6,250	6,710	210	1,840
1954	17,490	5,080	9,540	150	3,730
1955	25,660	5,900	14,210	250	10,230
1956	85,850	20,270	36,810	1,150	29,880
1957	65,330	14,920	26,020	1,060	31,730
1958	261,900	50,020	90,230	4,620	105,000

GROWTH OF STATE FARMS AND LIVESTOCK FARMS

	Unit	1949	1952	1957	1958
Farms	Number	18	404	710	1,442
Tractors	do	401	1,792	10,177	16,955
Combine harvesters	do	13	283	1,537	1,982
Lorries	do	28	229	3,444	4,284
Area used for production	thousand *mou*	460	8,480	17,990	39,820
Cultivated area	do	460	3,820	15,380	34,080
Reclaimed area	do	—	2,240	4,060	12,430
No. of workers and other employees	thousands	4	390	500	990

Note: Data include only the state farms and livestock farms under the Ministry of State Farms and Reclamation. The number of tractors is calculated on the basis of standard makes with 15-h.p.

INCREASING NUMBER OF TRACTORS USED FOR FARMING

	Number	Index numbers	
		1949=100	1952=100
1949	401	100	—
1950	1,286	320.7	—
1951	1,410	351.6	—
1952	2,006	500.2	100
1953	2,719	678.1	135.5
1954	5,061	1,260.0	252.3
1955	8,094	2,020.0	403.5
1956	19,367	4,830.0	965.5
1957	24,629	6,140.0	1,230.0
1958	45,330	11,300.0	2,260.0

Note: The tractors referred to here are of standard makes with 15-h.p.

GROWTH OF AGRICULTURAL SERVICES

(number of units)

	Agricultural technical stations	Livestock-breeding stations	Veterinary stations	Steppe development stations
1950	10	148	251	—
1951	43	274	576	—
1952	232	389	1,005	1
1953	3,632	578	1,734	7
1954	4,549	308	1,343	5
1955	7,997	454	1,266	4
1956	14,230	545	2,257	9
1957	13,669	821	2,930	23

GROWTH OF METEOROLOGICAL SERVICES

	Total	Meteorological observatories	Meteorological stations and weather forecasting stations
1949	101	5	96
1950	158	18	140
1951	191	19	172
1952	317	34	283
1953	357	43	314
1954	511	55	456
1955	715	67	648
1956	1,377	99	1,278
1957	1,647	110	1,537
1958	2,755	230	2,525

DEVELOPMENT OF AGRICULTURE AND LIVESTOCK BREEDING IN NATIONAL MINORITY AREAS

	Grain production (million catties)	Number of livestock in pastoral regions (thousand head)
1949	23,110	32,170
1952	31,630	...
1957	37,650	...
1958	53,090	65,640
(1949=100)		
1958	229.7	204.0

VI. RAPID DEVELOPMENT OF TRANSPORT AND POST AND TELE-COMMUNICATIONS

Considerable progress was made in transport and post and tele-communications in China during the past ten years to meet the growing needs of industry and agriculture.

In the early years after liberation, owing to damages caused by many years of war, communications and transport were practically paralysed, seriously hampering the exchange of commodities between cities and countryside and other places, adversely affecting industrial and agricultural production and the lives of the people. After the founding of the People's Republic of China, the work of restoring original lines of communications was successfully completed in a very short time and large-scale construction for communications began. During the seven years from 1952 to 1958 the Government appropriated no less than 13,200 million yuan on construction for communications and post and tele-communication facilities, a sum amounting to about 15.3 per cent of the Government's total investment in capital construction during that period.

As a result of the extensive building of communication facilities the backward state of transport in old China began to undergo great changes. By the end of 1958 the total length of railways actually in use was 31,193 kilometres, an increase of 42 per cent over 1949. The total length of highways was 400,000 kilometres, almost five times as much as existed in 1949. The total length of inland waterways was 150,000 kilometres, double the 1949 figure. Civil aviation lines had a total length of 33,000 kilometres, an increase of 190 per cent over the 1950 figure. Tibet, which in the past was known as a "forbidden area" for air travel, has long been accessible by plane. In addition, China-USSR, China-Mongolia, China-Vietnam, China-Korea and China-Burma air routes have also been opened. During the past ten years the volume of various means of transport has increased greatly. Compared with 1949, railway goods wagons increased 110 per cent by 1958, railway passenger carriages by 120 per cent, lorries by 120 per cent and the deadweight tonnage of merchant ships by more than 400 per cent.

As a result of the extensive development of communication facilities many original lines of transport were strengthened and many new lines were built. The state of extremely uneven distribution of communication lines, which prevailed in old China, began to undergo conspicuous changes. As we all know, in old China most of the railways and highways were built in the coastal regions and most of the transport facilities in the interior were exceedingly backward. Things are different now. The number of trunk railways and highways running through the extensive northwestern and southwestern China is multiplying and modern networks of communications and transport, covering the whole country, are being formed.

The rapid development of communications and transport has greatly facilitated the exchange of goods between the cities and the countryside and accelerated industrial and agricultural production. During the past ten years the goods carried by various means of transport and the freight turnover have increased remarkably. In 1958 goods carried by modern means of transport amounted to 630 million tons, an increase of 840 per cent over the 1949 figure, and the freight turnover was 236,400 million ton-kilometres, an increase of 930 per cent over the 1949 figure. Of these, in railway traffic, goods carried increased 580 per cent, and the ton-kilometres performed increased 910 per cent; in inland waterway transport and coastwise shipping, goods carried increased 1,310 per cent, and the ton-kilometres performed increased 920 per cent; in road transport, goods carried increased 2,940 per cent, and the ton-kilometres performed increased 2,660 per cent. Compared with pre-liberation peak figures the goods carried and ton-kilometres performed increased, in 1958, 80 per cent and 130 per cent respectively with regard to railway transport, 180 per cent and 70 per cent respectively with regard to water transport, and 1,130 per cent and 660 per cent respectively with regard to road transport.

With the rapid development of modern means of communications and transport in the past ten years, simple forms of transport in the countryside also enjoyed great progress. This was especially true during the big leap forward of 1958 when the rural people's communes, after having fulfilled their tasks with regard to field transport, allocated a huge amount of manpower and facilities to develop general transport. This greatly speeded up the transport of goods between cities and countryside and contributed to the big leap forward in industry and agriculture.

The efficiency of the various means of transport has increased in China during the past ten years. In comparison with 1949 the turn-round time of railway goods wagons in 1958 was shortened from 4.39 days to 2.75 days, a reduction of 37 per cent; the average daily distance covered by a railway goods wagon increased from 154.9 kilometres to 255.6 kilometres, an increase of 65 per cent; the average daily distance covered by a freight locomotive increased from 308.7 kilometres to 391 kilometres, an increase of 27 per cent; the average gross weight hauled by a freight locomotive increased from 1,011 tons to 1,704 tons, an increase of 69 per cent. In 1958 the daily efficiency per ton of capacity of lorries was 113 ton-kilometres, an increase of 530 per cent over the 1950 figure; the annual efficiency per ton of capacity of steamboats in coastwise shipping was 27,000 ton-knots, an increase of 61 per cent over 1952; the annual efficiency per ton of capacity of inland waterway steamboats was 51,000 ton-kilometres, an increase of 62 per cent over 1952; and the annual efficiency per horse-power of tug boats was 98,000 ton-kilometres, an increase of 190 per cent over the 1952 figure.

Because of the great enthusiasm for work and the creative genius of the broad masses of workers and other employees working in communications and transport and owing to the higher level of technical competence and the improved quality of equipment, the rate of labour productivity in communications and transport increased to a marked degree and transport costs continuously dropped. Compared with 1952 labour productivity increased in 1958 as follows: railway transport, more than 110 per cent, inland waterway transport, more than 220 per cent, coastwise shipping, more than 130 per cent. On the other hand railway transport costs dropped 25 per cent, inland waterway transport costs declined 51 per cent, and coastwise shipping costs declined 47 per cent.

During the past ten years speedy progress has also been made in post and tele-communications in China. In 1949 there were only approximately 20,000 post and telegraph offices in the whole country, but in 1958 the number had increased to more than 60,000. In 1958 the total length of postal routes was 3,012,000 kilometres, an increase of more than 300 per cent over the 1949 figure; the total length of long-distance tele-communication wires was 720,000 kilometres, an increase of 150 per cent over the 1949 figure; the national telephone trunk line capacity was 1.47 million, an increase of 290 per cent over the 1949 figure. By the end of 1958 as many as 98 per cent of the people's communes and 59 per cent of the production brigades of the people's communes could be reached by telephone. In 1958 the amount of business done in post and tele-communications in the whole country increased 250 per cent over the 1950 figure.

At present a network of post and tele-communications, with its centre in Peking, connecting all the provinces, municipalities, autonomous regions, special administrative regions, counties and people's communes, has been practically completed. A network of international tele-communications, with centres in Peking and Shanghai, connecting more than 30 countries, has also been established.

The great strides made by post and tele-communications accelerated industrial and agricultural production, especially during the big leap forward of 1958 when "telephone conferences" were frequently held. They played an important part in the timely exchange of experiences and in directing the big leap forward in industry and agriculture.

INCREASE IN LENGTH OF TRAFFIC LINES (I)

(kilometres)

	Railways	Highways	Inland waterways		Civil air routes
			Total	Of which: routes navigable by steamboat	
1949	21,989	80,768	73,615	24,182	...
1950	22,512	99,600	...	...	11,387
1951	23,352	114,428	...	...	10,497
1952	24,518	126,675	95,025	30,508	13,123
1953	25,072	137,103	...	...	13,971
1954	25,873	146,138	...	...	15,243
1955	27,171	167,282	99,938	31,685	15,511
1956	29,237	226,318	103,619	38,304	19,082
1957	29,862	254,624	144,101	39,194	26,445
1958	31,193	400,000	150,000	40,000	32,995

INCREASE IN LENGTH OF TRAFFIC LINES (II)

(index numbers)

	Railways	Highways	Inland waterways		Civil air routes
			Total	Of which: routes navigable by steamboat	
(1949=100)					
1952	111.5	156.8	129.1	126.2	115.2*
1957	135.8	315.3	195.7	162.1	232.2*
1958	141.9	495.2	203.8	165.4	289.8*
(1952=100)					
1957	121.8	201.0	151.6	128.5	201.5
1958	127.2	315.8	157.9	131.1	251.4
(1957=100)					
1958	104.5	157.1	104.1	102.1	124.8

* 1950 = 100.

RAPID INCREASE IN VOLUME OF GOODS CARRIED BY MODERN MEANS OF TRANSPORT (I)

(thousand tons)

	Total goods carried	Of which:		
		Carried by railways	Carried by motor vehicles	Carried by ships and barges
Pre-liberation peak	...	136,650	8,190	12,640
1949	67,130	55,890	5,790	5,430
1950	115,690	99,830	9,210	6,650
1951	135,060	110,830	14,120	10,110
1952	168,590	132,170	22,100	14,320
1953	212,270	161,310	30,940	20,010
1954	264,670	192,880	43,030	28,750
1955	278,430	193,760	48,960	35,700
1956	372,150	246,050	79,130	46,960
1957	411,710	274,200	83,730	53,770
1958	633,760	381,090	176,300	76,360

RAPID INCREASE IN VOLUME OF GOODS CARRIED BY MODERN MEANS OF TRANSPORT (II)

(index numbers)

	Total goods carried	Of which:		
		Carried by railways	Carried by motor vehicles	Carried by ships and barges
(Pre-liberation peak=100)				
1949	...	40.9	70.7	42.9
1952	...	96.7	269.7	113.4
1957	...	200.7	1,020.0	425.6
1958	...	278.9	2,150.0	604.3
(1949=100)				
1952	**251.1**	236.5	381.4	264.0
1957	**613.3**	490.6	1,450.0	991.0
1958	**944.1**	681.9	3,040.0	1,410.0
(1952=100)				
1957	**244.2**	207.5	378.9	375.3
1958	**375.9**	288.3	797.8	533.0
(1957=100)				
1958	**153.9**	139.0	210.6	142.0

RAPID INCREASE IN FREIGHT TURNOVER BY MODERN MEANS OF TRANSPORT (I)

(million ton-kilometres)

	Total freight turnover	Of which:		
		Performed by railways	Performed by motor vehicles	Performed by ships and barges
Pre-liberation peak	...	40,400	460	12,830
1949	22,980	18,400	250	4,310
1950	42,690	39,410	380	2,900
1951	59,340	51,560	570	7,210
1952	71,540	60,160	770	10,610
1953	93,010	78,140	1,300	13,570
1954	113,830	93,240	1;940	18,640
1955	125,120	98,150	2,520	24,440
1956	152,060	120,350	3,490	28,210
1957	172,930	134,590	3,940	34,390
1958	236,400	185,520	6,960	43,910

RAPID INCREASE IN FREIGHT TURNOVER BY MODERN MEANS OF TRANSPORT (II)

(index numbers)

	Total freight turnover	Of which:		
		Performed by railways	Performed by motor vehicles	Performed by ships and barges
(Pre-liberation peak=100)				
1949	...	45.5	54.9	33.6
1952	...	148.9	167.1	82.7
1957	...	333.1	859.0	268.1
1958	...	459.2	1,520.0	342.3
(1949=100)				
1952	**311.2**	327.0	304.4	246.0
1957	**752.4**	731.5	1,560.0	797.5
1958	**1,030.0**	1,010.0	2,760.0	1,020.0
(1952=100)				
1957	**241.7**	223.7	514.1	324.2
1958	**330.5**	308.4	908.1	413.9
(1957=100)				
1958	**136.7**	137.8	176.6	127.7

PASSENGERS CARRIED AND PASSENGER TURNOVER (I)

(absolute figures)

	Passengers carried (thousand persons)		Passenger turnover (million passenger-kilometres)	
	Total	Of which: carried by railways	Total	Of which: performed by railways
Pre-liberation peak	...	265,010	...	27,650
1949	134,940	102,970	15,410	13,000
1950	200,990	156,910	23,900	21,240
1951	219,860	160,370	26,850	23,050
1952	240,350	163,520	24,670	20,060
1953	350,010	228,610	34,820	28,170
1954	367,350	232,860	36,900	29,470
1955	361,250	208,010	35,190	26,740
1956	495,860	252,110	46,380	34,380
1957	622,710	312,620	49,490	36,130
1958	735,620	345,690	57,060	40,920

Note: The means of transport include railways, road motor vehicles, ships and barges and civil aviation aircraft.

PASSENGERS CARRIED AND PASSENGER TURNOVER (II)

(index numbers)

	Passengers carried		Passenger turnover	
	Total	Of which: carried by railways	Total	Of which: performed by railways
(Pre-liberation peak=100)				
1949	...	38.9	...	47.0
1952	...	61.7	...	72.6
1957	...	118.0	...	130.7
1958	...	130.4	...	148.0
(1949=100)				
1952	178.1	158.8	160.1	154.3
1957	461.5	303.6	321.2	277.9
1958	545.2	335.7	370.3	314.8
(1952=100)				
1957	259.1	191.2	200.6	180.1
1958	306.1	211.4	231.3	204.0
(1957=100)				
1958	118.1	110.6	115.3	113.3

PROGRESS IN CIVIL AVIATION

	Freight turnover (thousand ton-km.)	Passenger turnover (thousand passenger-km.)	Total flight hours for industrial and agricultural purposes (hours)
1. Absolute figures			
1950	820	9,780	—
1952	2,430	24,090	959
1957	8,250	79,870	9,168
1958	13,310	108,990	17,845
2. Index numbers			
(1950=100)			
1952	298.2	246.3	—
1957	1,010.0	816.4	956.0*
1958	1,630.0	1,110.0	1,860.0*

*1952 = 100,

EFFICIENCY OF LOCOMOTIVES AND GOODS WAGONS

	Unit	1949	1952	1957	1958
Average daily run per freight locomotive	km.	308.7	396.8	366.0	391.0[*]
Average gross weight hauled per freight locomotive	tons	1,011.2	1,245.3	1,520.2	1,704.0
Average daily efficiency per freight locomotive	thousand ton-km.	295.0	434.0	477.0	600.0
Coal consumption per freight locomotive per thousand ton-km.	kg.	25.2	19.5	14.6	14.8
Average turn-round time per goods wagon	days	4.39	2.90	2.84	2.75
Average turn-round distance per goods wagon	km.	668.7	676.1	709.2	703.6
Average daily run per goods wagon	km.	154.9	233.1	249.9	255.6
Average stopping time per goods wagon per run	hrs.	—	11.4	10.7	10.4
Average speed per freight train including stops	km./hrs.	19.9	25.5	25.2	25.7
Average load per goods wagon	tons	26.6	28.9	34.7	37.6
Average daily efficiency per goods wagon	ton-km.	2,509.0	4,557.6	5,999.0	6,596.0

[153]

EFFICIENCY OF LORRIES

	1950	1952	1957	1958
Percentage of lorries in serviceable condition	63.7	71.0	71.7	82.5
Percentage of lorries in actual use	30.1	39.5	66.3	77.9
Average daily run per lorry (kilometres)	79.8	109.2	162.2	174.3
Average daily efficiency per ton of capacity of lorries (ton-kilometres)	18	32	78	113

INCREASE IN LABOUR PRODUCTIVITY IN TRANSPORT

(percentage)

	1957 (1952=100)	1958 (1957=100)	1958 (1952=100)
Average amount of freight transported per person employed on railways	176.0	121.2	213.3
Average amount of freight transported per person employed in inland waterways	250.6	131.0	328.3
Average amount of freight transported per person employed in coastwise shipping	133.6	176.1	235.3

DECREASE OF UNIT COSTS IN STATE-OPERATED
TRANSPORT ENTERPRISES

(percentage)

	1957 (1952=100)	1958 (1957=100)	1958 (1952=100)
Railways	88.1	84.5	74.5
Inland waterways	60.5	80.5	48.7
Coastwise shipping	69.7	75.9	52.9

LENGTH OF POSTAL ROUTES AND TELE-COMMUNICATION WIRES AND VOLUME OF BUSINESS (I)

(absolute figures)

	Total length of postal routes (thousand km.)	Length of tele-communication wires (thousand kilometres)				Total vol. of business[1] (million yuan)
		Total	Long distance telephones	Intra-city telephones	Intra-county telephones	
Pre-liberation peak	748	561	468	93	—	—
1949	706	576	292	75	209	—
1950	863	653	308	80	265	166.4
1951	1,107	768	338	95	335	226.3
1952	1,290	882	365	111	406	243.5
1953	1,515	1,029	456	130	443	299.9
1954	1,640	1,138	487	152	499	327.8
1955	1,739	1,272	512	174	586	364.5
1956	1,811	1,856	564	216	1,076	431.4
1957	2,223	2,094	611	231	1,252	420.3
1958	3,012	3,202	719	301	2,182	553.9

[1]The total volume of business transacted in post and tele-communications up to and during 1957 was calculated in terms of the prices of 1952 and the statistics for 1958 were calculated in terms of the prices of 1957. These two sets of figures are not strictly comparable.

LENGTH OF POSTAL ROUTES AND TELE-COMMUNICATION WIRES AND VOLUME OF BUSINESS (II)

(index numbers)

	Total length of postal routes	Length of tele-communication wires				Total volume of business
		Total	Long distance telephones	Intra-city telephones	Intra-county telephones	
(Pre-liber-ation peak =100)						
1949	94.4	102.6	62.3	80.7	—	—
1952	172.5	157.1	78.0	118.4	—	—
1957	297.2	373.0	130.5	247.3	—	—
1958	402.8	570.6	153.7	322.6	—	—
(1949=100)						
1952	182.7	153.1	125.2	146.7	194.5	146.3*
1957	314.8	363.5	209.4	306.2	599.4	252.5*
1958	426.6	556.0	246.6	399.5	1,040.0	355.2*
(1952=100)						
1957	172.3	237.4	167.3	208.8	308.2	172.6
1958	233.6	363.1	197.0	272.4	537.1	242.8
(1957=100)						
1958	135.5	153.0	117.8	130.4	174.3	140.7

*1950 = 100.

[158]

RAPID DEVELOPMENT OF RURAL POST AND
TELE-COMMUNICATIONS

	1952	1953	1954	1955	1956	1957	1958
Postal routes in the countryside (thousand km.)	1,044	1,237	1,324	1,424	1,414	1,795	2,574
Percentage of towns and townships having postal service in relation to total number of towns and townships	59.0	65.1	75.2	78.2	96.1	99.0	100.0*
Percentage of towns and townships having telephones to the total number of towns and townships	9.4	13.0	14.9	19.3	62.0	69.3	97.7*

*Figures marked with an asterisk refer to people's communes.

DEVELOPMENT OF TRANSPORT AND POSTAL COMMUNICATIONS IN NATIONAL MINORITY AREAS

	Length of railways open to traffic (kilometres)	Length of highways open to traffic (kilometres)	Length of postal routes (kilometres)
1949	3,511	11,430	61,686
1952	3,787	25,648	131,262
1957	5,486	65,408	397,219
1958	6,353	94,879	549,204
(1949=100)			
1958	180.9	830.1	890.3

VII. EXPANSION OF DOMESTIC AND FOREIGN TRADE

On the basis of the rapid development of industrial and agricultural output and the uninterrupted increase in personal income, China's socialist trade has prospered as never before. The volume of commodity exchange has expanded conspicuously. In 1958 the volume of retail sales reached 54,800 million yuan, an increase of 16 per cent over 1957, or an increase of 221.2 per cent over 1950. The increases in the 1958 retail sales of some principal consumer goods as compared with 1950 were as follows: grain 62 per cent; edible vegetable oil 97.2 per cent; table salt 94.1 per cent; sugar 303.7 per cent; aquatic products 242.6 per cent; cotton cloth 124 per cent; rubber shoes 325 per cent; machine-made paper 270.7 per cent. These few figures show that the living standard of the people has risen considerably.

In the past ten years socialist trade has effectively aided the rapid development of industrial and agricultural production through the purchase of industrial and agricultural products, the supply of capital goods for industrial and agricultural production, the expansion of commodity exchange between town and country, the stabilization of market prices and other means. In 1958 the total value of industrial products purchased by the state trading organizations and the supply and marketing co-operatives reached 32,600 million yuan, while purchases of agricultural products and products of agricultural subsidiary occupations amounted to 18,800 million yuan, representing respective increases of 280 per cent and 190 per cent over 1952. The trading departments supply the industrial departments with large quantities of capital goods to ensure the rapid expansion of industrial production, and at the same time they supply agriculture with the means of production in ever increasing quantities. In 1958 the value of the means of production supplied to the countryside reached 6,700 million yuan, 4.7 times as much as in 1952. In the seven years between 1952 and 1958 the principal items supplied included: 9,230,000 tons of chemical fertilizer; 25,230,000 tons of different kinds of oil cakes; 930,000 tons of insecticides; 6,500,000 insecticide sprayers; power machines totalling 1,630,000 horsepower; 2,270,000 two-wheeled share ploughs; 2,670,000 iron water-wheels; 39,250,000 spades; etc. Such large quantities of supplies to the countryside have played an important part in expanding agricultural production.

In ten years, trade in the areas inhabited by national minorities has developed remarkably. In 1958 the volume of retail sales in these areas reached 4,690 million yuan, 2.6 times that of 1952.

Since March 1950, market prices have remained stable. In the early period of liberation, the influence of the habitual runaway inflation that existed during the reactionary Kuomintang regime and the wild activities of speculative capital caused a steady rise in prices. This seriously affected the normal industrial and agricultural production and the stability of the people's life. Confronted by such a situation, the People's Republic of China, soon after its establishment, concentrated on stabilizing market prices. The People's Government quickly centralized control of finance and economy throughout the country, took active steps to balance revenue and expenditure and strengthened state control of cash funds. It also dealt severe blows to speculative business practices and then banned them, rapidly established and developed state commerce, centralized control and allocation of important material resources related to the national welfare and the people's daily needs and ensured a flow of supplies to the market. In less than six months, starting from March 1950, the prices which had been rising constantly for more than a decade were brought under virtual control and market prices were basically stabilized. Taking March 1950 as 100, the index number for wholesale prices throughout the country in December 1950 was 85.4; in 1951 it was 92.4; and in 1952 it was 92.6. Again taking March 1950 as 100, the index numbers for retail prices in eight cities including Peking, Shanghai and Tientsin were as follows: December 1950, 83.9; 1951, 94.6; 1952, 93.7. This rapid stabilization of prices not only contributed to the improvement of the people's living conditions, but also provided important conditions for the speedy rehabilitation and development of the national economy.

After the virtual stabilization of prices in the whole country, the state systematically raised the purchasing prices for a number of agricultural products during the period of the First Five-Year Plan, with the aim of reducing the disparity between prices for industrial and agricultural products which existed before liberation, so as to encourage the peasants to produce more. Because of these higher prices and because retail prices of industrial goods sold in rural areas remained practically unchanged, the disparity of prices between industrial and agricultural products was reduced considerably, the incomes of the peasants increased and their living conditions improved. Calculations show that during the First Five-Year Plan, the higher prices that the state paid for agricultural products resulted in an increase in the peasants' incomes by the total sum of 11,000 million yuan.

The stabilization of market prices in March 1950 was followed by basic changes in the character of China's market. From a market controlled by bureaucrat-capital and engaged in speculation and other activities disruptive to the national economy, it became a market under the guidance of the socialist state economy and served in the development of the national economy.

There has been a remarkable expansion in China's foreign trade in the past ten years. In 1958 China's total volume of import and export trade amounted to 12,870 million yuan,

3.1 times that of 1950. Of this figure the volume of imports increased 2.9 times and the volume of exports increased 3.3 times. With the establishment of the People's Republic of China, the semi-colonial character of old China's foreign trade and century-old unfavourable balance of trade and deficits in balance of payments have gone for ever.

China's foreign trade serves her socialist construction, her industrial and agricultural production and the improvement of the people's standard of living. During these ten years, of all the goods imported, more than 90 per cent were in the category of capital goods required for construction. Agricultural products still constituted the principal exports. With the development of industrial production, however, the proportion of exports of industrial and mining products has gradually risen from 9.3 per cent in 1950 to 27.5 per cent in 1958.

With equality and mutual benefit as the basis of her foreign trade policy, China has developed trade and commercial relations with the fraternal socialist countries and friendly governments and peoples. In ten years, trade between China and the Soviet Union and other socialist countries has increased considerably. The total volume of imports and exports in 1958 was 6.5 times that of 1950; with imports registering a 5.6 times increase and exports 7.5 times. Such trade has been carried on on the basis of mutual aid, co-operation, equality, mutual benefit and mutual promotion of economic development. It is a completely new pattern of trade relations.

Soon after the founding of the People's Republic of China, U.S. imperialism, persisting in its hostile policy towards the Chinese people, carried out its "blockade" and "embargo" against China, in an attempt to disrupt New China's economic construction. This policy, however, failed long ago. Those who were really hurt by the "blockade" and "embargo" were the countries which followed U.S. imperialism in implementing that policy, not the Chinese people

China's trade with Asian and African countries which is based on equality and mutual benefit has markedly expanded

[164]

in the ten years; the total volume of import and export trade has doubled from 1950 to 1958. Since 1953 China's trade with Western countries has increased to a certain extent.

In 1958 China concluded trade agreements with more than 20 countries and established economic and trade relations with more than 90 countries and regions.

INCREASE IN VOLUME OF RETAIL SALES

	Total retail sales (million yuan)	Index numbers		
		1950=100	1952=100	Preceding year=100
1950	17,060	100	—	—
1951	23,430	137.3	—	137.3
1952	27,680	162.3	100	118.1
1953	34,800	204.0	125.7	125.7
1954	38,110	223.4	137.7	109.5
1955	39,220	229.9	141.7	102.9
1956	46,100	270.2	166.5	117.5
1957	47,420	278.0	171.3	102.9
1958	54,800	321.2	198.0	115.6

INCREASE IN RETAIL SALES OF PRINCIPAL COMMODITIES

	Retail sales in 1950	Retail sales in 1958	1958 (1950=100)
Grain	55,510 million catties	89,950 million catties	162.0
Edible vegetable oil	1,080 million catties	2,130 million catties	197.2
Table salt	2,061,000 tons	4,000,000 tons	194.1
Pork	1,400,000 tons	1,764,000 tons	126.0
Aquatic products	721,000 tons	2,470,000 tons	342.6
Sugar	243,000 tons	981,000 tons	403.7
Cotton cloth	2,170 million metres	4,860 million metres	224.0
Rubber shoes	41,927,000 pairs	178,190,000 pairs	425.0
Matches	6,500,000 bales[1]	11,914,000 bales	183.3
Machine-made paper	140,000 tons	519,000 tons	370.7

[1] One bale contains 1,000 boxes.

INCREASE IN PURCHASE OF AGRICULTURAL PRODUCTS AND PRODUCTS OF AGRICULTURAL SIDE-OCCUPATIONS

	Total purchased (million yuan)	Index numbers		
		1950=100	1952=100	Preceding year=100
1950	8,000	100	—	—
1951	10,500	131.3	—	131.3
1952	12,970	162.1	100	123.5
1953	15,320	191.5	118.1	118.1
1954	17,360	217.0	133.8	113.3
1955	17,800	222.5	137.2	102.5
1956	18,400	230.0	141.9	103.4
1957	20,280	253.5	156.4	110.2
1958	22,760	284.5	175.5	112.2

INCREASE IN PURCHASE OF PRINCIPAL AGRICULTURAL PRODUCTS AND PRODUCTS OF AGRICULTURAL SIDE-OCCUPATIONS

	Unit	Amount purchased in 1950	Amount purchased in 1958	1958 (1950=100)
Grain	million catties	66,850	105,920	158.4
Edible vegetable oil	do	1,130	1,760	155.8
Pigs	thousand head	35,843	46,732	130.4
Eggs	thousand tan	3,279	8,100	247.0
Tea	do	1,194	2,409	201.8
Cotton	do	8,226	30,598	372.0
Cured tobacco	do	1,028	5,530	537.9

Notes: 1. Figures for grain, cotton and edible vegetable oil include taxes in kind.
2. Edible vegetable oil includes oil-yielding plants in terms of amount of oil extracted.

INCREASE IN TOTAL AMOUNT OF MEANS OF PRODUCTION SUPPLIED TO AGRICULTURE

	Total amount (million yuan)	Index numbers		
		1950=100	1952=100	Preceding year=100
1950	730	—	—	—
1951	1,030	141.1	—	141.1
1952	1,410	193.2	100	136.9
1953	1,920	263.0	136.2	136.2
1954	2,500	342.5	177.3	130.2
1955	2,820	386.3	200.0	112.8
1956	3,700	506.8	262.4	131.2
1957	3,260	446.6	231.2	88.1
1958	6,680	915.1	473.8	204.9

INCREASE IN QUANTITY OF MAJOR ITEMS OF MEANS OF PRODUCTION SUPPLIED TO AGRICULTURE

	Chemical fertilizer (thousand tons)	Insecticide (thousand tons)	Insecticide sprayers (thousand units)	Two-wheeled share ploughs (thousand units)	Power machines (thousand horse-power)
1. Quantity supplied					
1952	318	15	251	1	13
1953	592	19	198	15	14
1954	802	41	315	23	22
1955	1,255	67	429	426	45
1956	1,608	159	1,308	1,086	189
1957	1,944	149	647	95	265
1958	2,708	478	3,351	628	1,083
2. Index numbers					
(1952=100)					
1957	611.3	993.3	257.8	9,500.0	2,000.0
1958	851.6	3,200.0	1,300.0	62,800.0	8,300.0
(1957=100)					
1958	139.3	320.8	517.9	661.1	408.7

COMMODITY PRICE INDEX NUMBERS (I)

(nation-wide. Average prices of the preceding year = 100)

	Wholesale prices	Retail prices	Purchasing prices for agricultural products	Retail prices of industrial products in the countryside
1952	100.1	99.9	101.7	99.5
1953	98.7	103.2	110.1	98.5
1954	100.4	102.2	103.4	101.7
1955	100.6	100.8	99.5	101.2
1956	99.5	100.0	103.0	99.0
1957	100.9	102.2	105.0	101.2
1958	100.0	99.7	102.2	99.4

COMMODITY PRICE INDEX NUMBERS (II)

(nation-wide. Average 1952 prices = 100)

	Wholesale prices	Retail prices	Purchasing prices for agricultural products	Retail prices of industrial products in the countryside
1953	98.7	103.2	110.1	98.5
1954	99.1	105.5	113.8	100.2
1955	99.7	106.3	113.2	101.4
1956	99.2	106.3	116.6	100.4
1957	100.1	108.6	122.4	101.6
1958	100.1	108.3	125.1	101.0

Note: The slight increases in retail prices were mainly due to the fact that non-staple foods were priced too low in the past, necessitating readjustments every year. The rise in purchasing prices for agricultural products was due to the unreasonable disparity of prices between industrial and agricultural products in the past. Planned readjustments have been made in the past years.

COMMODITY PRICE INDEX NUMBERS (III)

(average March 1950 prices = 100)

	Wholesale prices, nation-wide	Retail prices in eight major cities
1951	92.4	94.6
1952	92.6	93.7
1953	91.3	98.3
1954	91.8	100.2
1955	92.4	101.1
1956	91.9	101.0
1957	92.7	102.2
1958	92.7	101.4

RAPID INCREASE OF TRADE IN NATIONAL MINORITY AREAS

(million yuan)

	1952	1958	1958 (1952=100)
Volume of retail sales	1,790	4,690	262.0
Volume of sales by state trading companies and co-operatives	770	4,400	568.6
Value of agricultural products and products of agricultural side-occupations purchased	750	2,020	269.3
Value of purchases by state trading companies and co-operatives	480	2,930	616.4

RAPID INCREASE IN VOLUME OF IMPORT AND EXPORT TRADE

	Total volume of import and export trade (million yuan)	Index numbers	
		1950=100	Preceding year=100
1950	4,150	100.0	—
1951	5,950	143.2	143.2
1952	6,460	155.5	108.6
1953	8,090	194.8	125.2
1954	8,470	203.9	104.7
1955	10,980	264.3	129.6
1956	10,870	261.5	98.9
1957	10,450	251.5	96.2
1958	12,870	309.8	123.2

VOLUME OF IMPORT AND EXPORT TRADE BY CATEGORY

(percentage distribution)

	Imports (total=100)		Exports (total=100)		
	Capital goods	Consumer goods	Industrial & mining products	Processed products of agriculture and side-occupations	Products of agriculture and side-occupations
1950	87.2	12.8	9.3	33.2	57.5
1951	83.1	16.9	14.0	31.4	54.6
1952	90.6	9.4	17.9	22.8	59.3
1953	93.0	7.0	18.4	25.9	55.7
1954	92.8	7.2	24.0	27.7	48.3
1955	94.5	5.5	25.5	28.4	46.1
1956	92.4	7.6	26.1	31.3	42.6
1957	92.7	7.3	28.4	31.5	40.1
1958	93.7	6.3	27.5	37.0	35.5

VIII. UNPRECEDENTED INCREASE IN THE NUMBER OF WORKERS AND OTHER EMPLOYEES

With the rapid expansion of the national economy in the past ten years, the ranks of the working class have swollen as never before. Unemployment, a hang-over from old China, has disappeared.

Immediately after liberation, one of the chief tasks in the cities was the gradual solution of the problem of unemployment, a problem inherited from the reactionary Kuomintang government. When the People's Republic was established, the state took over several million employees from the former Kuomintang military, administrative, public and educational organizations. Even so, there were about four million unemployed and a still larger number of young people who had never been employed and had been unable to continue their studies, housewives and other employable people. Although the problem of mass unemployment could not be solved in old China, the People's Republic has satisfactorily solved it in less than ten years. By the end of 1957 the number of workers and other employees actually working reached 24,510,000, more than triple the figure of eight million at the end of 1949. The number was further increased to 45,320,000 by the end of 1958 as a result of the great leap forward in the national economy. This was 20 million more than the number employed at the end of 1957. By this time the unemployment left over from the old days had disappeared. With the setting up of the people's communes in all rural areas, household chores have been gradually taken over by community services, releasing tens of millions of women from drudgery and enabling them to take part in social labour, thus greatly reinforcing the labour force. Day by day the number of employed has increased. The elimination of unemployment in China is a glaring contrast to the ever-growing army of unemployed in capitalist countries, eloquent testimony to the superiority of the socialist system over the capitalist system.

In the course of the past ten years the state adopted a series of measures aimed at simplifying administrative offices. The personnel in non-productive work was reduced, while the personnel in productive work was increased. From 1949 to 1958 the proportion of the personnel in productive departments rose from 65 per cent of the total number employed to 85 per cent, while the proportion of the personnel in the non-productive departments decreased from 35 per cent to 15 per cent. The rapid increase in the personnel in productive departments ensures the speedy advance of production and construction.

The Party and Government have attached great importance to the education and training of cadres, technical personnel, new workers and apprentices. Many of them have been educated and trained in schools, special courses and actual practice in enterprises. From 1949 to mid-1959, eight million apprentices were trained, of whom 5,400,000 have already completed their apprenticeship. The technical schools have trained 270,000 students, of whom over 200,000 have already graduated. The number of engineering and technical personnel in China reached 618,000 in 1958, 3.8 times the number in 1952.

During the rectification campaign in 1957, the Party and Government decided to send cadres to the countryside or factories so that they may take part in manual work and learn through labour. Each cadre was called upon to spend some time each year doing manual work so as to come into closer contact with the masses. From 1957 to 1958 more than a million cadres have gone to the countryside, factories or mining enterprises to engage in manual labour, so that they may combine mental work with manual work and come into closer touch with the masses. At the same time, industrial and mining establishments instituted a system of having the cadres take part in labour and the workers take part in management. The three-way co-operation between management, technical personnel and the workers has served to popularize experiences in technological reform. As a result, the enthusiasm of the workers was greatly aroused and production increased.

Through vigorous socialist emulation campaigns and the movements for increasing production and practising economy, which were launched by the broad masses of workers and other employees over the last ten years, a large number of outstanding workers and outstanding groups have continuously emerged. Taking the statistics of the trade unions alone, the number of model workers who were selected after comparison by the trade unions on the primary level exceeded 2,440,000 in 1958, and the number of outstanding groups reached 200,000. In the nine years between 1950 and 1958, 31,960,000 rationalization proposals were submitted by the workers and other employees in industrial and mining enterprises throughout the country. These proposals have been put into practice and have either saved or earned large sums for the state and have effectively accelerated the rapid expansion of production and construction.

CONTINUOUS INCREASE IN NUMBER OF WORKERS AND OTHER EMPLOYEES (I)

(thousand persons)

	Number at year-end	Increase over preceding year	Increase over 1949
1949	8,004	—	—
1950	10,239	2,235	2,235
1951	12,815	2,576	4,811
1952	15,804	2,989	7,800
1953	18,256	2,452	10,252
1954	18,809	553	10,805
1955	19,076	267	11,072
1956	24,230	5,154	16,226
1957	24,506	276	16,502
1958	45,323	20,817	37,319

Notes: 1. The number of workers and other employees for 1958 includes those employed in newly opened industrial establishments at the county level and below and the workers and other employees in those industrial and commercial enterprises, grain agencies and cultural and educational organizations which the state transferred to the people's communes.

2. The average number of workers and other employees in 1958 was 32,000,000, an increase of about 8,000,000 over 1957.

[180]

CONTINUOUS INCREASE IN NUMBER OF WORKERS AND OTHER EMPLOYEES (II)

(index numbers)

	1949=100	1952=100	Preceding year=100
1950	127.9	—	127.9
1951	160.1	—	125.2
1952	197.5	100	123.3
1953	228.1	115.5	115.5
1954	235.0	119.0	103.0
1955	238.3	120.7	101.4
1956	302.7	153.3	127.0
1957	306.2	155.1	101.1
1958	566.3	286.8	184.9

INCREASE IN NUMBER OF FEMALE WORKERS

	Number (thousand persons)	Index numbers		
		1949=100	1952=100	Preceding year=100
1949	600	100	—	—
1952	1,848	308.0	100	—
1953	2,132	355.3	115.4	115.4
1954	2,435	405.8	131.8	114.2
1955	2,473	412.2	133.8	101.6
1956	3,266	544.3	176.7	132.1
1957	3,286	547.7	177.8	100.6
1958	7,000	1,166.7	378.8	213.0

RAPID INCREASE IN NUMBER OF INDUSTRIAL WORKERS

	Number (thousand persons)	Index numbers		
		1949=100	1952=100	Preceding year=100
1949	3,004	100	—	—
1952	4,939	164.4	100	—
1953	6,188	206.0	125.3	125.3
1954	6,408	213.3	129.7	103.6
1955	6,477	215.6	131.1	101.1
1956	8,626	287.2	174.7	133.2
1957	9,008	299.9	182.4	104.4
1958	25,623	853.0	518.8	234.4

Note: Data do not include apprentices.

INCREASE IN ENGINEERING AND TECHNICAL PERSONNEL

	Number (thousand persons)	Index numbers	
		1952=100	Preceding year=100
1952	164	100.0	—
1953	210	128.0	128.0
1954	262	159.8	124.8
1955	344	209.8	131.3
1956	449	273.8	130.5
1957	496	302.4	110.5
1958	618	376.8	124.6

RAPID INCREASE IN PERCENTAGE OF WORKERS AND OTHER EMPLOYEES IN PRODUCTIVE WORK

(total = 100)

	Productive work	Non-productive work
1949	65.0	35.0
1950	60.9	39.1
1951	63.8	36.2
1952	66.1	33.9
1953	67.7	32.3
1954	68.7	31.3
1955	68.5	31.5
1956	72.2	27.8
1957	72.9	27.1
1958	85.1	14.9

NUMBER OF OUTSTANDING GROUPS AND WORKERS

	Outstanding groups (thousands)		Outstanding workers (thousand persons)	
	Total	Of which: outstanding teams	Total	Of which: female
1949-1952	19	18	208	26
1953	15	14	155	21
1954	17	14	234	19
1955	21	18	316	33
1956	114	81	1,259	113
1957	106	78	1,078	103
1958	199	136	2,441	281

IX. TREMENDOUS PROGRESS IN CULTURE AND EDUCATION

In the past decade the Chinese people have scored unprecedented achievements in the field of culture in keeping with their great achievements in economic construction. Culture, education and the arts developed and flourished, particularly during the big leap forward in 1958. The literacy campaign and a mass movement encouraging the people to run schools by themselves engulfed the country and the people's cultural life became richer and more colourful. As Chairman Mao Tse-tung said: "With the upsurge in economic construction, there will inevitably appear an upsurge of cultural construction." His prediction has come true.

Education in New China is fundamentally different from old China. The new policy is: education to serve the political interests of the proletariat and education to be combined with productive labour. Guided by this correct policy China has made tremendous strides in education during the past decade. Enrolment in primary schools, middle schools and institutes of higher learning increased several fold. Literacy classes and spare-time general and technical education developed greatly. The system of combining education with productive labour and the work-while-you-study programme have been put into practice. Large numbers of cadres have been trained for socialist construction.

In 1958 the number of students in higher educational institutes reached 660,000, 5.7 times the number in 1949 and more than four times the pre-liberation peak. In that year there were 1,470,000 students in technical middle schools, 6.4 times the 1949 figure and 3.8 times the pre-liberation peak, while the students in middle schools numbered 8,520,000, 8.2 times the 1949 figure and 5.7 times as many as in the pre-liberation peak year. There were 86,400,000 primary school pupils in 1958, 3.5 times the number in 1949 and 3.6 times the pre-liberation peak. In 1958, universal primary school education was put into effect in many counties; 85 per cent of all school-age children were in school in the country as a whole.

In the ten years from 1949 to 1958, 430,000 students graduated from institutes of higher learning, more than double the total number of graduates in the 20 years before liberation. The number of graduates from engineering colleges and departments in the same period was 130,000, four times the total number of graduates in the 20 years before liberation. In ten years New China had 1,300,000 graduates from technical middle schools, more than double the total number of graduates in the 16 years before liberation.

Spare-time study for peasants, workers and other employees developed considerably in the past decade. The literacy campaign has been popularized among the masses. During the big leap forward in 1958, in particular, industrial and mining enterprises and people's communes opened a large number of spare-time schools, with an attendance of more than 30 million. Illiteracy was wiped out among 40 million people, more than the total number in the preceding nine years. At the same time, large numbers of workers, peasants and soldiers become interested in studying Marxist-Leninist theory. A high tide of studying philosophy was set in motion by the masses.

Education in China belongs to the working people. In the past ten years, as the material life of the working people improved steadily, many more worker's children enrolled in schools. The proportion of students from worker and peasant families in the various types of schools has increased year by year. In higher educational institutes, students from worker and peasant families constituted 19 per cent of the student body in 1951. In 1958 they increased to 48 per cent of the student body. In the technical middle schools, students of worker and peasant origin accounted for 57 per cent of the students in 1951 and 77 per cent in 1958. Students from worker and peasant families constituted 51 per cent of the student body in middle schools in 1951 and 75 per cent in 1958.

In the past decade, China's science, culture and the arts, guided by the policy of "let a hundred flowers blossom and a hundred schools of thought contend," carried on and developed the fine national traditions. Culture and science flourished. In 1957 there were 580 institutes of scientific research and more than 28,000 research and technical personnel throughout China, more than triple the number in 1952. Scientific research developed even more rapidly in the big leap forward of 1958. It became more integrated with productive labour, resulting in a mass interest in science, which in turn stimulated large numbers of working people to invent countless new devices. By the end of 1958, the number of institutes of scientific and technological research in the country increased more than 21 times and the number of research and technical personnel increased more than 51 times in comparison with pre-liberation days. In 1958, elementary scientific research bureaux were established in about half the counties and municipalities in China. Special institutes for scientific research were established by many industrial and mining enterprises. An atomic reactor of heavy water type and a cyclotron were built in 1958. The rapid development of scientific research paved the way for China to catch up with the world's advanced levels of science and technique.

The past ten years witnessed unprecedented activity in China's publishing, cinema, drama, song and dance, broadcasting and other fields of culture and art. Between 1950 and 1958, the circulation of newspapers increased from 800 million copies to 3,900 million copies, 4.9 times as many; journals increased from 35 million copies to more than 530 million copies, 15 times as many; and the number of books published increased from 270 million to 2,390 million, 8.7 times as many. Between 1949 and 1958, the number of feature films made or dubbed in Chinese rose from 9 to 178, an increase of 20 times; the number of film projection units rose from 646 to 13,000, more than 19 times as many. There were more than 6,700 wire broadcasting stations in 1958, 21 times the 327 stations which existed in 1952. More than 5,000 of these were rural people's commune wire broadcasting stations. A broadcasting network in the countryside has thus been established in the main. Television stations were set up in Peking and Shanghai in 1958. In addition, many cultural centres, cultural stations and public libraries were established by the state as well as by the people themselves. Opera and drama have flourished.

Sports have been organized on a mass scale and the level of performance has risen considerably. All the records set in old China have been broken and higher records are constantly being set. World records were set in 16 events including weight-lifting, track and field, swimming, parachute jumping, mountain climbing, shooting and model aeroplane flying. China won the 1959 world table tennis championship for men's singles.

The past decade saw considerable development in culture and education among China's national minorities. In 1958, the national minorities had 4,240,000 pupils in primary schools, 4.5 times the number in 1951; 395,000 middle school students, 9.8 times the 1951 figure; and 22,000 students in institutes of higher learning, 10.6 times the number in 1951. By 1959, the state had helped create written languages for ten national minorities which had never had a written language before. Many national minorities now have books, journals and newspapers published in their own languages. In the seven years from 1952 to 1958, books published in national minority languages included more than 9,000 titles in more than 80 million copies. More than 30 periodicals and an equal number of newspapers were published in the languages of the national minorities throughout China in 1958. Cultural halls and stations, dramatic groups, film projection teams, libraries, book stores and wire broadcasting stations were established on a wide scale. Many national minorities now have their own writers, educators and scientific workers.

NUMBER OF ENROLLED STUDENTS (I)

(thousands)

	Institutes of higher learning	Technical middle schools	Middle schools	Primary schools
Pre-liberation peak year	155	383	1,496	23,683
1949	117	229	1,039	24,391
1950	137	257	1,305	28,924
1951	153	383	1,568	43,154
1952	191	636	2,490	51,100
1953	212	668	2,933	51,664
1954	253	608	3,587	51,218
1955	288	537	3,900	53,126
1956	403	812	5,165	63,464
1957	441	778	6,281	64,279
1958	660	1,470	8,520	86,400

Note: A large number of agricultural middle schools and other vocational middle schools were opened in 1958, with an enrolment of two million students. The figures for students in institutes of higher learning given here and elsewhere do not include research students.

NUMBER OF ENROLLED STUDENTS (II)

(index numbers)

	Institutes of higher learning	Technical middle schools	Middle schools	Primary schools
(1949=100)				
1952	164.1	277.7	239.7	209.5
1957	378.7	339.9	604.6	263.5
1958	566.2	642.3	820.0	354.2
(1952=100)				
1957	230.8	122.4	252.2	125.8
1958	345.1	231.2	342.2	169.1
(1957=100)				
1958	150.0	188.9	135.6	134.4
(Pre-liberation peak year=100)				
1958	426.6	384.1	569.6	364.8

NUMBER OF GRADUATES (I)

(thousands)

	Institutes of higher learning	Technical middle schools	Middle schools	Primary schools
Pre-liberation peak year	25	73	326	4,633
1949	21	72	280	2,387
1950	18	75	296	2,829
1951	19	57	284	4,232
1952	32	68	221	5,942
1953	48	118	454	9,945
1954	47	169	644	10,136
1955	55	235	969	10,254
1956	63	174	939	12,287
1957	56	146	1,299	12,307
1958	72	191	1,313	16,225

NUMBER OF GRADUATES (II)

(index numbers)

	Institutes of higher learning	Technical middle schools	Middle schools	Primary schools
(1949=100)				
1952	149.9	95.0	79.1	248.9
1957	263.1	203.6	463.5	515.7
1958	339.2	265.9	468.6	679.8
(1952=100)				
1957	175.6	214.4	586.3	207.1
1958	226.3	280.0	592.7	273.1
(1957=100)				
1958	128.9	130.6	101.1	131.8
(Pre-liberation peak year=100)				
1958	288.6	260.2	402.6	350.2

NUMBER OF GRADUATES FROM INSTITUTES OF HIGHER LEARNING

	Engineering	Agriculture	Economics and finance	Medicine	Natural sciences	Pedagogy	Liberal arts
Pre-liberation peak year	4,792	2,064	2,969	1,236	1,701	3,250	2,736
1949	4,752	1,718	3,137	1,314	1,584	1,890	2,521
1950	4,711	1,477	3,305	1,391	1,468	624	2,306
1951	4,416	1,538	3,638	2,366	1,488	1,206	2,169
1952	10,213	2,361	7,263	2,636	2,215	3,077	1,676
1953	14,565	2,633	10,530	2,948	1,753	9,650	3,306
1954	15,596	3,532	6,033	4,527	802	10,551	2,683
1955	18,614	2,614	4,699	6,840	2,015	12,133	4,679
1956	22,047	3,541	4,460	5,403	3,978	17,243	4,025
1957	17,162	3,104	3,651	6,200	3,524	15,948	4,294
1958	17,499	3,513	2,349	5,393	4,645	31,595	4,131

Note: Data include only the main faculties of the institutes of higher learning. In the pre-liberation peak year series, the faculty of agriculture includes the faculty of forestry, and the faculty of pedagogy includes the faculty of physical culture.

COMPARISON OF NUMBER OF GRADUATES FROM INSTITUTES OF HIGHER LEARNING BEFORE AND AFTER LIBERATION

(thousands)

	20 years before liberation (1928–1947)	10 years after liberation (1949–1958)	1949–1958 (1928–1947=100)
Total	**185**	**431**	**232.5**
Of which:			
Engineering	32	130	408.9
Agriculture	13	26	234.9
Forestry		5	
Medicine	9	39	410.8
Natural sciences	16	23	148.4
Pedagogy	21	104	507.0
Physical culture		3	

Note: The total number of graduates from the technical middle schools during the ten years after liberation reached 1,305,000, accounting for 238.7 per cent of the 547,000 graduates during the sixteen years (1931-1946) before liberation.

NUMBER OF PEOPLE ATTENDING SPARE-TIME SCHOOLS AND NUMBER OF THOSE NEWLY LITERATE

(thousands)

	Spare-time institute of higher learning	Spare-time technical middle schools	Spare-time middle schools	Spare-time primary schools	Newly literate
1949	0.1	0.1	...	...	657
1950	0.4	0.1	...	...	1,372
1951	1.6	0.3	...	...	1,375
1952	4.1	0.7	249	1,375	656
1953	9.7	1.1	404	1,523	2,954
1954	13.2	186.0	760	2,088	2,637
1955	15.9	195.0	1,167	4,538ʼ	3,678
1956	63.8	563.0	2,236	5,195	7,434
1957	75.9	588.0	2,714	6,267	7,208
1958	150.0	—	5,000	26,000	40,000

INCREASE IN NUMBER OF NATIONAL MINORITY STUDENTS

	Institutes of higher learning	Technical middle schools	Middle schools	Primary schools
1. Absolute figures (thousands)				
1951	2	5	40	943
1952	3	19	73	1,474
1953	6	26	137	2,546
1954	8	24	160	2,465
1955	9	23	169	2,468
1956	14	33	234	3,152
1957	16	37	277	3,194
1958	22	64	395	4,240
2. Index numbers				
(1951=100)				
1958	1,060	1,230	979.6	449.5

Note: Research students are included in the figures for students in institutes of higher learning.

PROPORTION OF STUDENTS OF WORKER AND PEASANT ORIGIN TO TOTAL NUMBER OF STUDENTS

(percentage of total in each category)

	Institutes of higher learning	Technical middle schools	Middle schools
1951	19.1	56.6	51.3
1952	20.5	57.1	56.1
1953	21.9	55.9	57.7
1954	...	58.8	60.7
1955	29.0	62.0	62.2
1956	34.1	64.1	66.0
1957	36.3	66.6	69.1
1958	48.0	77.0	75.2

Note: Data for students in institutes of higher learning include research students.

PROPORTION OF FEMALE STUDENTS TO TOTAL NUMBER OF STUDENTS

(percentage of total in each category)

	Institutes of higher learning	Technical middle schools	Middle schools	Primary schools
Pre-liberation peak year	17.8	21.1	20.0	25.5
1949	19.8	...	...	...
1952	23.4	24.9	23.5	32.9
1957	23.3	26.5	30.8	34.5
1958	23.3	27.0	31.3	38.5

INCREASE IN KINDERGARTENS

(thousands)

	Number of kindergartens	Number of children in kindergartens	Number of teachers
1. Absolute figures pre-liberation peak year	1.3	130	2
1950	1.8	140	2
1952	6.5	424	14
1957	16.4	1,088	42
1958	695.3	29,501	1,193
2. Index numbers			
(Pre-liberation peak year=100)			
1958	53,400	22,700	55,700
(1950=100)			
1958	38,600	21,000	69,200

SCIENTIFIC RESEARCH INSTITUTES AND PERSONNEL (1958)

	Number of institutes	Personnel (thousands)	
		Total	Of which: research & technical personnel
Total	**848**	**118.6**	**32.5**
Of which: Basic science	170	28.3	5.9
Industry and communications	415	59.2	14.7
Agriculture, forestry, animal husbandry and fishery	134	10.8	1.2
Medical science and public health	101	12.1	2.2

Note: Data cover the institutes of natural sciences and technology under the various ministries of the Central People's Government, provinces, municipalities directly under the central authority, autonomous regions, seven municipalities and the Chinese Academy of Sciences. Institutes of philosophy, social sciences, literature and the arts are not included.

ACTIVITIES OF THE ASSOCIATION FOR THE DISSEMINATION OF SCIENTIFIC AND TECHNICAL KNOWLEDGE

(thousand events)

	1952	1957	1958
Lectures	13.8	629.5	214,538
Exhibitions	0.5	15.8	79.9
Films and lantern slide shows	4.5	52.4	18.9

NUMBER OF CULTURAL HALLS, PUBLIC LIBRARIES AND MUSEUMS

	Cultural halls	Public libraries	Museums
1949	896	55	21
1950	1,693	63	22
1951	2,226	66	31
1952	2,448	83	35
1953	2,441	93	49
1954	2,392	93	46
1955	2,413	96	50
1956	2,584	375	67
1957	2,748	400	72
1958	2,616	922	360

Note: Data do not include the cultural halls, public libraries and museums in the people's communes.

GROWTH OF CINEMA INDUSTRY

	Number of films produced or dubbed in Chinese	Film projection units	Of which:	
			Cinemas	Projection teams
1. Absolute figures				
1949	9	646	596	—
1952	43	2,282	746	1,110
1957	119	9,965	1,030	6,692
1958	178	12,579	1,386	8,384
2. Index numbers				
(1949=100)				
1952	477.8	353.3	125.2	100.0
1957	1,322.2	1,542.6	172.8	602.9*
1958	1,977.8	1,947.2	232.6	755.3*

*1952 = 100.

NUMBER OF DRAMATIC GROUPS AND THEATRES

	Dramatic groups	Theatres
1950	1,676	1,083
1952	2,017	1,562
1957	2,808	2,358
1958	3,162	2,620

INCREASE IN CIRCULATION OF PRINTED MATTER

(million copies)

	Newspapers	Journals	Books
1.Absolute figures			
1950	797.5	35.3	274.6
1952	1,609.0	204.2	785.7
1957	2,442.4	315.0	1,278.0
1958	3,912.8	532.4	2,389.3
2.Index numbers			
(1950=100)			
1952	201.7	578.6	286.1
1957	306.3	892.3	465.4
1958	490.6	1,508.2	870.0

Note: Data cover only the newspapers, journals and books published at special administrative region level and above.

NUMBER OF WIRE BROADCASTING STATIONS AND LOUDSPEAKERS

	Wire broadcasting stations	Loudspeakers (thousands)
1949	8	0.5
1950	51	2.2
1951	183	6.1
1952	327	16.2
1953	541	31.8
1954	577	47.5
1955	835	90.5
1956	1,490	515.7
1957	1,700	993.2
1958	6,772	2,987.5

POPULARIZATION OF SPORTS AMONG THE MASSES
(end of 1958)

Number of ·people who fulfilled physical culture requirements under
the manual labour and national defence programme 25,570,000

Number of qualified sportsmen 4,106,000

Number of masters of sports (end of August 1959) 1,044

NUMBER OF WORLD RECORDS CREATED
(end of August 1959)

	Number of people	Number of events	Number of records
Total	**33**	**16**	**26**
Weight-lifting	3	4	11
Swimming	2	1	3
Track and field events	1	1	1
Shooting	1	1	1
Parachute jumping	15	6	7
Mountain climbing	9	1	1
Model aeroplane flying	2	2	2

Note: By August 1959, 1,362 sportsmen had broken 2,805 national records in
various events. All national records made before liberation have been
broken.

DEVELOPMENT OF THE CULTURE OF THE NATIONAL MINORITY PEOPLES

	Unit	1952	1957	1958	1958 (1952=100)	1958 (1957=100)
Film projection units	number	155	1,097	1,559	1,005.8	142.1
Of which:						
Cinemas	do	75	136	184	245.3	135.3
Projection teams	do	61	868	1,198	1,963.9	138.0
Newspapers (in minority languages)	thousand	29,330	24,340	39,800	135.7	163.5
Journals (in minority languages)	do	1,690	2,440	3,600	213.5	147.7
Books (in minority languages)	do	6,610	14,620	23,880	361.1	163.4

X. GREAT IMPROVEMENT IN THE LIVING STANDARD OF THE PEOPLE

On the basis of the growth of production, the Chinese people's living standard has risen greatly in the past decade.

Wages for workers and other employees have been increasing steadily. During the period of the rehabilitation of the national economy, from 1949 to 1952, the average wage increase for workers and other employees throughout the country was as high as 70 per cent. In the First Five-Year Plan period the increase was 42.8 per cent. Average wages in 1958, not including wages for new workers and other employees, registered a further increase of 3 per cent over 1957. At the same time family incomes of the workers and other employees were higher in 1958 than in 1957 as a result of increased employment.

In addition to raising wages the state has shown great concern for the daily needs and welfare of the workers and employees. Shortly after the founding of the People's Republic of China labour insurance was introduced for workers in factories and mining enterprises throughout the country. Free medical services were extended to government functionaries and personnel in people's organizations and schools, thus eliminating their difficulties caused by childbirth, old age, sickness, disablement and death, problems which could hardly be avoided in old China. In 1958, 13,780,000 workers and other employees were covered by labour insurance, 4.2 times the 3,300,000 people covered in 1952. Again in 1958, 6,880,000 workers and other employees were entitled to free medical services as against 4,000,000 in 1952, a 72 per cent increase. To further raise the incomes of the workers and other employees and improve their welfare, the state spent 14,100 million yuan in the seven years from 1952 to 1958 for labour insurance, free medical services, subsidies for culture and education, bonuses and other welfare services.

The living conditions of the workers and other employees improved markedly in the past decade. In the seven years from 1952 to 1958 alone, the investment by the state on housing for workers and other employees amounted to 6,300 million yuan for 128 million square metres of floor space. In other words, on the basis of the average number of workers and other employees over the seven-year period, the state spent more than 290 yuan per worker for an average of six square metres of new housing. This is unprecedented in the history of old China, nor has this ever happened or can it possibly happen in capitalist countries.

In comparison with pre-liberation days the standard of living of the Chinese workers and other employees has risen a great deal. According to statistics, in 1936, the year before the War of Resistance to Japanese Aggression, the per capita annual consumption expenditures of workers and other employees (including their family members) amounted to 140 yuan.* It rose to 189.5 yuan* in 1952 and again rose to 227 yuan* in 1958. The 1952 figure was 35 per cent higher and the 1958 figure was 62 per cent higher than that of 1936, proof of the outstanding material improvements socialism has brought to the Chinese workers.

China's peasants, numbering over 500 million, have also enjoyed a marked improvement in their standard of living as a result of the continued rise of agricultural output. During the period of the rehabilitation of the national economy, from 1949 to 1952, the income of peasants throughout China increased more than 30 per cent in general. During the First Five-Year Plan period it again increased almost another 30 per cent. During the great leap forward of agricultural pro-

---

* At 1957 prices.

duction in 1958 the peasants' lives improved even more. Their 1958 incomes showed an increase of more than 10 per cent over 1957. Total rural purchasing power reached about 30,000 million, an increase of 20 per cent over 1957 and 80 per cent over 1952. Compared with 1952, the increases in per capita purchases of major consumer goods by peasants in 1958 were as follows: grain, 18 per cent; edible vegetable oil, 62 per cent; aquatic products, 180 per cent; table salt, 18 per cent; sugar, 100 per cent; cigarettes, 82 per cent; cotton cloth, 25 per cent; cotton knitwear, 100 per cent; rubber shoes, 240 per cent; soap, 160 per cent; water flasks, 680 per cent; machine-made paper, 130 per cent; kerosene, 170 per cent; and coal, 150 per cent. A rising level of consumption by peasants on such a scale is unparalleled in China's history; it would have been impossible in the past.

With the rise in income, bank deposits in the cities and in rural areas have multiplied.

The past decade witnessed rapid progress in public health service. The health of the labouring people has improved. In 1958 there were more than 5,600 hospitals and sanatoria throughout the country with 440,000-odd beds, an increase of 2.1 times and an increase of 5.2 times respectively in comparison with 1949. In addition, there were established a large number of medical centres and clinics, health stations for women and children, anti-epidemic stations, mobile anti-epidemic teams, medical centres and stations for special purposes as well as other health institutes. The people's communes in the countryside set up many health centres in 1958 during the big leap forward. Now every commune has a hospital and each production brigade has a clinic and a maternity station.

As a result of the extensive promotion of the mass movement for sanitation and the campaign to wipe out the four "evils," the number of flies, mosquitoes, rats, grain-eating sparrows and other pests has been greatly reduced and hygiene in towns and in the countryside has improved. Smallpox, bubonic plague and other serious contagious diseases, which in the past jeopardized the people's health, have been eradicated in the main. Before liberation cholera was prevalent in China, but not a single case occurred in the past ten years. Kala-azar has been practically wiped out in the area north of the Yangtse River where it used to be rampant and schistosomiasis is under control in many areas where it had been common.

In 1958, the technical personnel in public health service throughout the nation totalled 2,160,000, more than double the 1952 figure. Among them were 75,000 doctors trained in Western medical science, a 46 per cent increase over 1952, and about 500,000 doctors trained in Chinese traditional medicine. The medical heritage of China has developed greatly in recent years, thanks to the unity and co-operation of Western-trained and traditional doctors. The level of our medical science has improved.

Public health services in the national minority areas have made considerable progress in the past ten years. Up to the end of 1958 there were 750 hospitals with more than 31,900 beds and 25 sanatoria with more than 2,300 beds. There were 15,000 medical centres, clinics, anti-epidemic stations and mobile anti-epidemic teams staffed by 179,000 health workers and technical personnel. Due to the development of the economy, culture, education and public health, the population of the national minorities has increased and their health needs are taken care of. The common progress and prosperity of the nationalities in China and their fraternal unity present a striking contrast to the national oppression and racial discrimination in capitalist countries. This further demonstrates the superiority of socialism.

From the above figures and simple facts, we can see clearly that while China is carrying on large-scale economic construction, the people's living standard has risen continuously. On the occasion of the tenth anniversary of the People's Republic of China, the 650 million Chinese people have expressed their joy at the brilliant success achieved in socialist revolution and socialist construction and the great improvement in their lives. High in spirits and firm in determination, they work hard and are advancing towards a further fundamental change of the "poverty and blankness" left over from the past, towards a beautiful future and a peaceful and happy life.

INCREASE IN AVERAGE ANNUAL WAGE OF WORKERS AND OTHER EMPLOYEES

	Average annual wage (yuan)	Index numbers	
		1952=100	Preceding year=100
1952	446	100	—
1953	496	111.2	111.2
1954	519	116.4	104.6
1955	534	119.7	102.9
1956	610	136.8	114.2
1957	637	142.8	104.4
1958	656	147.1	103.0

Note: The figure for the 1958 average wage is calculated on the basis of the number of workers and other employees employed in 1957. It does not include those newly employed in 1958.

RAPID INCREASE IN INCOME OF PEASANTS

(index numbers, 1952 = 100)

1953	106.9
1954	110.7
1955	120.7
1956	124.3
1957	127.9
1958	142.9

HOUSING FLOOR SPACE FOR WORKERS AND OTHER EMPLOYEES BUILT BY THE STATE

(thousand square metres)

	Floor space of new housing built each year	Accumulated total floor space of new housing
1950	2,510	2,510
1951	4,600	7,110
1952	7,510	14,620
1953	13,420	28,040
1954	13,270	41,310
1955	14,460	55,770
1956	25,230	81,000
1957	28,160	109,160
1958	26,420	135,580

NUMBER OF WORKERS AND OTHER EMPLOYEES COVERED BY LABOUR INSURANCE

	Absolute figures (thousand persons)	Index numbers	
		1949=100	Preceding year=100
1949	600	100	—
1950	1,400	233.3	233.3
1951	2,600	433.3	185.7
1952	3,300	550.0	126.9
1953	4,830	805.0	146.4
1954	5,380	896.7	111.4
1955	5,710	951.7	106.1
1956	7,417	1,236.2	129.9
1957	11,500	1,916.7	155.0
1958	13,779	2,296.5	119.8

Note: Data do not include those covered by collective agreements.

NUMBER OF WORKERS AND OTHER EMPLOYEES COVERED BY FREE MEDICAL CARE

	Absolute figures (thousand persons)	Index numbers	
		1952=100	Preceding year=100
1952	4,000	100	—
1957	6,572	164.3	—
1958	6,877	171.9	104.6

INCREASE IN URBAN SAVINGS DEPOSITS

	1950=100	Preceding year=100
1950	100	—
1951	416.5	416.5
1952	655.0	157.3
1953	925.4	141.3
1954	1,082.4	117.0
1955	1,286.7	118.9
1956	1,697.0	131.9
1957	2,119.4	124.9

INCREASE IN NUMBER OF BEDS IN HOSPITALS AND SANATORIA

	Absolute numbers (thousand beds)	Index numbers	
		1949=100	Preceding year=100
Pre-liberation peak year	66	—	—
1949	84	100	—
1950	106	126.1	126.1
1951	134	159.1	126.2
1952	180	214.7	134.9
1953	215	256.4	119.4
1954	250	297.7	116.1
1955	279	332.2	111.6
1956	328	390.9	117.7
1957	364	433.4	110.9
1958	440	524.4	121.0

Note: Data do not include the 922,000 second grade beds which were available in 1958 in various public health institutions throughout the country, more than ten times the number in 1957.

DEVELOPMENT OF PUBLIC HEALTH SERVICES FOR WOMEN AND CHILDREN

	Unit	Pre-liberation peak year	1949	1952	1957	1958
Maternity hospitals[1]	number	81	80	98	96	230
No. of beds	do	1,736	1,762	4,052	6,794	7,557
Children's hospitals	do	3	5	6	16	27
No. of beds	do	173	139	258	2,295	3,682
Health stations for women and children	do	9	9	2,379	4,599	4,315
Permanent child-care organizations[2]	thousands	0.1	0.3	2.7	17.7	3,186.3
Children under care[3]	do	· —	13	99	488	47,140

[1] Excluding maternity clinics established in the countryside by the people's communes. By the end of 1958 their number reached 134,000 with 416,000 beds.
[2], [3] 1958 figures include the people's communes.

INCREASE IN NUMBER OF PERSONS WORKING IN PUBLIC HEALTH SERVICES

| | Total number | Of which: | | | Midwives |
		Western-trained doctors	Doctor's assistants	Nurses	
1. Absolute figures (thousand persons)					
1950	780	41	53	38	16
1952	1,040	52	67	61	22
1957	1,908	74	136	128	36
1958	2,160	75	131	138	35
2. Index numbers					
(1950=100)	100	100	100	100	100
1952	133.3	125.0	124.5	161.1	142.7
1957	244.7	177.7	254.1	339.1	227.9
1958	276.9	182.0	245.5	364.8	224.8
(1952=100)	100	100	100	100	100
1957	183.5	142.2	204.1	210.5	159.7
1958	207.7	145.6	197.1	226.4	157.5

Note: Doctors of Chinese traditional medicine, totalling about half a million throughout the country, are not included.

DEVELOPMENT OF PUBLIC HEALTH SERVICES IN NATIONAL MINORITY AREAS

	Unit	1954	1957	1958	1958 (1954=100)	1958 (1957=100)
Hospitals	number	443	603	750	169.3	124.4
Beds	do	9,428	20,773	31,983	339.2	154.0
Sanatoria	do	7	17	25	357.1	147.1
Beds	do	403	1,277	2,302	571.2	180.3
Clinics and health stations	do	1,453	5,541	14,230	979.4	256.8
Anti-epidemic stations and teams	do	24	175	281	1,170.8	160.6
Mobile anti-epidemic teams	do	44	60	70	159.1	116.7